Love Covers Over

Endorsements for *Love Covers Over*

Love Covers Over is a rich resource for Christian parents. It's not only practical and easy to follow, but comprehensive in its coverage of LGBTQ+ topics, providing the knowledge and tools needed to foster love, acceptance, and faith within your family.

Dr. Douglas Jacoby
International Bible Teaching Ministry

Love Covers Over is the compassionate and truthful guide parents need. Without fear, anger, or condemnation, Radcliff graciously shares her personal experience in the LGBTQ+ community and shows how Christian parents can move forward with love, not fear.

Phylicia Masonheimer
Every Woman a Theologian

Ellen's ability to distill complex and emotional subjects into easily digestible insights is remarkable. *Love Covers Over* is a must-read for any Christian parent seeking clarity and guidance on LGBTQ+ matters.

Guy Hammond
Executive Director of Strength in Weakness Ministries

A must-read for every Christian parent. Ellen compiles real, current life struggles facing our children today and graciously approaches each question with deep, Christlike compassion and biblical conviction. *Love Covers Over* is sure to serve as a guide to the anxious and curious on how to parent with wisdom and love while also considering the relevant psychology and theology.

Brenna Blain
Contemporary Theologian and Author

In this most important book *Love Covers Over*, Ellen wonderfully describes how parents can rise above only correcting their child's behavior and instead, seek to reach their hearts. I earnestly ask every Christian parent to read this book. God bless you, Ellen, for sharing your expertise and insights— every Christian parent desperately needs the help you are so graciously and effectively offering.

Gordon Ferguson
Gordon Ferguson Teaching Ministry

You will come away from *Love Covers Over* having great hope and clarity in your own worldview and mindset as a Christian full of Christ's love while holding to a Biblical sexual ethic, and also having the practical ideas and skills that are so important in being who Christ is calling you to be to your struggling children. Definitely recommended.

Dr. Carol Tanksely
Dr. Carol Ministries

love covers over

A GUIDE FOR CHRISTIAN PARENTS
RAISING KIDS IN AN LGBTQ+ WORLD

Ellen Radcliff, LMFT, LCMHC

NASHVILLE

NEW YORK • LONDON • MELBOURNE • VANCOUVER

Love Covers Over

A Guide for Christian Parents Raising Kids in an LGBTQ+ World

Published in New York, New York, by Morgan James Publishing. Morgan James is a trademark of Morgan James, LLC. www.MorganJamesPublishing.com

All Scripture quotations, unless otherwise indicated, are taken from the Holy Bible, New International Version®, NIV®. Copyright ©1973, 1978, 1984, 2011 by Biblica, Inc.® Used by permission of Zondervan. All rights reserved worldwide. www.zondervan.com The "NIV" and "New International Version" are trademarks registered in the United States Patent and Trademark Office by Biblica, Inc.®

Scripture quotations marked (HCSB) are taken from the Holman Christian Standard Bible, copyright © 1999, 2000, 2002, 2003, 2009 by Holman Bible Publishers, Nashville Tennessee. All rights reserved.

Scripture quotations marked (NKJV) are taken from the New King James Version®, copyright © 1982 by Thomas Nelson. Used by permission. All rights reserved.

Scripture quotations marked (NLT) are taken from the Holy Bible, New Living Translation, copyright ©1996, 2004, 2015 by Tyndale House Foundation. Used by permission of Tyndale House Publishers, Carol Stream, Illinois 60188. All rights reserved.

Scripture quotations marked (NIRV) are taken from the New International Reader's Version, copyright © 1995, 1996, 1998, 2014 by Biblica, Inc.®. Used by permission. All rights reserved worldwide.

Proudly distributed by Publishers Group West®

Morgan James BOGO™

A **FREE** ebook edition is available for you or a friend with the purchase of this print book.

CLEARLY SIGN YOUR NAME ABOVE

Instructions to claim your free ebook edition:
1. Visit MorganJamesBOGO.com
2. Sign your name CLEARLY in the space above
3. Complete the form and submit a photo of this entire page
4. You or your friend can download the ebook to your preferred device

ISBN 9781636983790 paperback
ISBN 9781636983806 ebook
Library of Congress Control Number:
2024941116

Cover Design by:
Roy AMDesigns

Interior Design by:
Chris Treccani
www.3dogcreative.net

Morgan James is a proud partner of Habitat for Humanity Peninsula and Greater Williamsburg. Partners in building since 2006.

Get involved today! Visit: www.morgan-james-publishing.com/giving-back

Dedication

This book is dedicated to my parents,

who never gave up on me,

and to my children, who have fueled my desire

to examine God's perfect love in parenting.

Contents

Preface

When I was first introduced to Hebrews 4:13, I was twelve years old with an ever-growing ache in my heart to be fully seen, known, and loved. I remember reading the terrifying words, "Everything is uncovered and laid bare before the eyes of him to whom we must give account."

My preteen heart couldn't help but equate this to the kind of vulnerability and exposure that exists in romantic love. I felt fear mixed with impossible hope in the potential of one day finding true love that contained this level of intimacy. I knew that the love I longed for would mean being fully exposed before another—something that terrified me to my core, even then.

I convinced myself that exposing myself at the level Hebrews 4:13 required would quickly collapse any romantic feelings someone could possibly have for me. But there was a small whisper in my heart that wondered if it was possible for me to be fully exposed before another and still be loved and accepted.

Little did I know that this wasn't a sexual or romantic awakening beginning in my heart; this was my heart stirring to the kind of all-encompassing love that only God can provide. Not fully understanding this at the time, I embarked on a quest to seek the kind of intimacy I yearned for but dared not fully hope for.

I had no romantic prospects at the time, so I began my search for connection in friendships. Because the lines are so easily blurred between romantic love and platonic love, especially for women, I quickly found myself emotionally entangled with a female friend.

This emotional entanglement led to a physical relationship and a lesbian identity. Though this took the edge off my internal ache to find a Hebrews 4:13 kind of intimacy, it did not completely fulfill my deep desire to be fully seen, known, and understood.

Years of confusion, heartache, and searching led me back to God, where I finally got to experience the Hebrews 4:13 intimacy that I had dreamed of since my youth—but not without scars from my search. To help salve these scars, I embarked on another quest, a search to understand my experience with my sexuality and gender identity. That quest led me to a master's degree in counseling and to becoming a marriage and family therapist and clinical mental health counselor.

I have had the honor of wrestling through LGBTQ+ topics both in my own life and alongside others as they walk this path. If you are on this path, whether by yourself or with someone else, I pray this book will be helpful to you as you wrestle with some of these topics before God.

Love Covers Over

It is inspiring to watch someone live out their faith obediently. I had the privilege of seeing that every day of my early life. When I was three years old, my parents devoted their lives to Christ. Watching them wrestle, struggle, fall, repent, obey, and surrender before the Lord time and again has personally refined me.

My parents never set an expectation of perfection; they set an expectation of *repentance*. They will be the first to tell you that they are not perfect parents (with all respect and love, I concur). However, they are the perfect parents for me (and for my three younger brothers, one near my age and two that came along much later). Their goal was not to be perfect parents, but to strive toward love.

One late night, during his early days of parenting, my dad was reflecting on a vow that he had made to God when he was nine years old—to not be like his own dad. At this tender age, my father made a pact with a

God whom he did not yet intimately know and vowed to be the type of father that he had always wanted, the type of father that he deserved—an involved and loving father who took a vested interest in his children and their upbringing.

On that late night of reflection, Dad started ruminating over all the mistakes he had made as a parent thus far and all the future mistakes that were bound to happen. He began to wonder if the vow that he made at nine was possible for him to carry out. As he considered his imperfection as a parent, weary from self-condemnation, teetering on the brink of hopelessness, and searching for guidance on how to fulfill this sensitive, aged vow, he came across 1 Peter 4:8: "Above all, love each other deeply, because *love covers over a multitude of sins*" (emphasis added).

Relief washed over Dad as he felt a surge of joy—the aid he had been searching for since he was nine years old was finally revealed to him! He had discovered the key to *imperfect* parenting!

He ran downstairs, Bible in hand, and with a childlike delight, breathlessly exclaimed to my mom, "Honey! I found it! I know how we're going to get through this parenting thing! We're gonna love…as hard as we can. As much as we can. When we don't know what to do, we're just going to love them!"

The long-awaited answer: *Love covers over.* Love is the salve that soothes imperfections in parenting.

There were many times growing up when my parents did not have the right answers, when they didn't know what to do or say, and when they felt lost. But the anchor that held them and kept them confident and rooted in God was love—their love for God, their love for their children, and God's love for our family.

What to Expect

I am forever grateful for the imperfect parenting that I received from my parents and for the perfect parenting that I receive from God every day. It is these experiences with both my heavenly Parent and my earthly parents, my own experience in parenting, my experience as a former lesbian, and my experience as a marriage and family therapist that I draw on to share how love can cover over when you are navigating LGBTQ+ topics in our culture, in your home, or maybe with your child.

As you wade through this book, you will enter into what I like to call the *messy middle space*. The messy middle is a space where we strive toward both unconditional love AND unwavering righteousness. A space that Jesus pioneered, championed, and staunchly upheld. A space that holds to biblical truth but does so with revolutionary love and grace. If you do not hold to the traditional biblical sexual ethic, this book may not be for you. Likewise, if your goal is to change your child's sexual or gender identity, this is not the book you're looking for.

Instead, this book will help Christian parents navigate the intimidating topics of sex, sexuality, and gender with their children through a biblical lens, free of fear and shame. This book will also help Christian parents with LGBTQ+ children to maintain connection with their child, even during disagreement over LGBTQ+ topics. As we dive into more of the technical aspects of the development of sexual orientation and gender identity, I hope you will reflect on your own upbringing as you empathize with individuals (maybe even your own child) experiencing some of these delicate struggles.

As you read this book, you might feel an urge to rush toward precise answers to your specific and urgent questions. However, these delicate questions do not have swift, one-size-fits all answers. Instead, they demand a robust understanding of God, relationships, personal growth, emotional processing, and effective communication. Once this foundation is firmly established, specific answers to your questions will become more evident. I encourage you to sit back and immerse yourself in the information as we construct the essential groundwork for addressing your questions effectively.

In Part 1 we will explore an overview of developmental stages pertinent to gender and sexual identity, along with foundational parenting principles to guide children toward a relationship with God at every stage of their growth. In Part 2 we will unpack necessary constructs that serve as avenues with which to create the time, space, and connection needed to discuss difficult topics, like LGBTQ+ discussions. Part 3 seeks to reclaim God's intent for sex, sexuality, and gender, aiming to dispel certain misconceptions that have had a negative impact on us all and prepare parents to teach their children about these tender topics. Part 4 contains psychologically informed, spiritually grounded, and practical advice tailored for Christian parents of LGBTQ+ children. Parents will receive specific guidance on how to create and maintain deep connections to their LGBTQ+ child and communicate around their LGBTQ+ identity in a way that honors both the child and the parents' faith. And then finally, the appendices include a unique perspective from my own parents and frequently asked questions, offering insights into some of the most pressing concerns Christian parents have regarding LGBTQ+ topics.

I hope to equip you with tools to guide you through parenting your child(ren) in an LGBTQ+ world while standing firmly, with Jesus, in the messy middle space. I have found it's impossible to do that without some personal refinement, as every one of us experiences brokenness in the areas of sex, sexuality, and gender. The "Reflect and Discuss" questions may help you refine and align your perspective of these areas with God's. Only then can we as parents better prepare our children for life in a confused world while remaining rooted in Christ.

If you are reading this book as part of a parent support group, the questions at the end of each chapter can help guide your group discussion. If you are reading this book on your own, consider answering these questions by journaling or by talking them through with God, a spouse, a therapist, or a trusted friend.

Disclaimers

I recognize the multitude of perspectives present in this complex discussion. Addressing these sensitive topics can feel like tiptoeing through a minefield. While I'm eager to share my thoughts, I am also mindful of choosing my words carefully to ensure that they articulate the heart behind them. Yet, despite my best efforts to convey my views thoughtfully, misunderstandings may result. Let me clarify a few key points from the outset:

LGBTQ+ experiences: I use this term throughout the book to describe individuals who identify with any aspect of the LGBTQ+ spectrum.

LGBTQ+ identities: I use this term to describe individuals who identify with any aspect of the LGBTQ+ spectrum and prioritize that identity over their faith, such as being in a same-sex romantic relationship or living as a gender incongruent with their natal sex. I acknowledge that some Christians interpret the biblical sexual and gender ethic differently, viewing their LGBTQ+ identity not as a prioritization over their faith. When discussing these individuals in this book, I will indicate their distinctive theological perspective.

Biological sex vs. gender: Throughout the book I use the terms "gender" and "biological sex" interchangeably, unless specifically defining them based on current cultural perceptions. I will give the basis for my reasoning within the book, and while I understand that many do not agree that both terms mean the same thing, I assure you that it is never my intention to disrespect those whose views diverge from mine on this or any other point of controversy. Additionally, at times, I utilize the term "sex" to refer to the physical act of love. In that section I will use the term "gender" synonymously with "biological sex" to avoid confusion. However, a comprehensive explanation of these terms is provided in Chapter 11 (and referenced in Chapters 2 and 10 and in Appendix 3).

Crossing gender boundaries: Some may take exception with me not defining what constitutes crossing gender boundaries and what does not. But the scope of this book is not to define where the gender boundaries lie according to God. I did not write this book with the intention of telling parents what they should or should not let their children do. The purpose of the book is to help Christian parents determine where their *own* conscience lies in regard to each nuanced decision around LGBTQ+ topics, and then to help them communicate that clearly, lovingly, and effectively to their children.

PART 1

Beyond Paradise:
Parenting in a Fallen World

Before we can determine how best to help our children navigate LGBTQ+ topics, we first must understand what is happening with them developmentally. This section will highlight some of the prominent characteristics of three different stages of development: early childhood (ages 4–6), middle childhood (ages 7–11), and early adolescence (ages 12–18).[1] Each characteristic explored in this section could play a role in the development of sexual orientation or gender identity. Distortions in each of these developmental stages exist because of one common factor that all of humanity suffers from—growing up outside Eden.

This part of the book does not provide definitive explanations for LGBTQ+ experiences, nor does it offer guidance on how to prevent an LGBTQ+ identity in your child. It is not intended to induce guilt in parents whose children have already gone through these stages. Instead, it aims to satisfy parents' desire to know about the kinds of potential factors that could contribute toward an LGBTQ+ identity. Ultimately, the goal of this part is to highlight the complexity of the origins of LGBTQ+ identities in the hopes of fostering a surrendered approach in parents' hearts, rather than one laden with self-blame, as many of these potential factors lie outside a parent's control. While modern science suggests that both biological and environmental influences contribute to most characteristics a human experiences, including LGBTQ+ identities, this discussion focuses solely on potential environmental (or "nurture") factors, as the biological aspects fall outside the scope of this book.

Chapter 1:

Outside Eden

My best friend Tina noticed a change in her one-year-old daughter, Josephine. Her sweet, innocent baby had morphed, seemingly overnight, into a demanding, attention-hungry, petulant toddler. Tina, frustrated that she couldn't even quickly turn her attention to something else without eliciting protesting wails from Josephine, became increasingly desperate for some explanation as to why her daughter needed a level of constant love, affection, and attention that she was incapable of offering. After prayer, advice, and meditation before God, Tina had an epiphany: Josephine wasn't made for the love of this world. *None of us were.*

We were all created for a perfect, all-consuming love that can only come from God. We were created for Eden, where we would abide with God and where 100 percent of our identity and worth would come from him and his perfect love. But then we were each thrust into a broken world. We still have access to God and his love, but not in the same way that we were created for. So we walk around with this huge, gaping hole in our hearts, searching for the type of fulfillment that we long for, that we were created for, but having to settle for the type of pseudo-fulfillment and worth that the world offers us.

We were meant to come into this world and look first into God's perfect eyes and see our reflection through him—a reflection that mirrored back someone wholly and perfectly loved, adored, and sought after by the Creator of the universe. Instead, being born into a post-Edenic world, we first look into the imperfect eyes of our parents. Eyes that love us, to be sure! Eyes that are doing the best they can with what they have. But eyes that have been equally broken and distorted by the pain that naturally exists in a world outside Eden. We are all—you, me, and our children—living in the harsh realities of this broken world. A reality that creates distortions in how we see and understand ourselves, God, truth, love, and worth.

The good news is that we have found him! The source of our love, identity, and fulfillment. We know where to look to find that part of us that was created in Eden. And our ultimate goal as parents is not to get our kids to behaviorally comply with our faith; our goal is not to get them to profess their faith and devotion to God by a certain age; our goal is not even to protect them from all the pain and distortion of this broken world (unfortunately, that is not possible). Our ultimate goal is to give them but a glimpse into who God is by our example in love and parenting.

We will, of course, do this imperfectly, as we are affected by the brokenness of this world, just like our kids. But the good news is that *love covers over* a multitude of sins (1 Peter 4:8). Your love for your child will cover over a multitude of your shortcomings. And God's perfect love for you, your children, and your family can cover over a multitude of your imperfections as a parent.

Parental Surrender

Seeing the effects that a fallen world has on our children can be devastating and terrifying. Fear can tend to rule over us and become our motivation in how we parent. But this is a distorted representation of God's love to our children. We are not called to parent and discipline our children out of fear, but out of love—just like God does with us. When fear takes over our parenting, we tend to either (1) attempt to control too much in our children's lives—things we don't really have control over in the first place or (2) freeze up, do nothing, and bury our heads in the sand because it's all too overwhelming. Though both reactions are understandable in the wake of fear and grief, they are not going to serve us or our children well in parenting, especially as it relates to LGBTQ+ topics.

Therefore, parenting is one big, lifelong exercise in surrender. Surrendering is perhaps the hardest thing we do as parents because it involves encountering some very difficult things: (1) confronting our fear, (2) grieving that we don't have the control that we want to over the situation, (3) actively turning our children over to God, (4) trusting God, even without fully understanding him, and (5) persevering by getting back up to fight.

Surrender is often the point of our deepest pain and fear before God. But this is what is needed to do our jobs well as parents. We must continually put our children in the hands of God, relinquishing full control over them.

Stewards

My favorite word to use in this discussion with parents is "steward." It correctly conveys the appropriate level of surrender we need to have as we parent our children. The Bible is clear that we are to love our kids, protect them as much as we have control over, and discipline them—teach and train them in the ways of the Lord. But we are meant to do this as *stewards*. Our children belong to us; but God is their ultimate Creator and Keeper. We are proxies on this earth for God, even with our kids—proxy parents, proxy protectors, proxy providers, and proxy teachers.

This ought to fill Christian parents with a certain level of relief that we can relinquish full control over our kids to God. But being God's steward to our children should also fill us with deference. We ought to quake in reverent fear as we realize that we are the closest representative of God in our children's lives.

I don't know about you, but when I'm relaxing at home after a long day, it's often easy to "clock out" from being God's representative. There are many times that the worst version of me comes out around my family. But this is so backward! Reflect on how much God loves your child(ren) and on how important the parent-child relationship is to him. He uses a parent-child metaphor throughout Scripture to give us a glimpse into the kind of loving, fiercely protective, and actively adoring Father he is. And our children will learn about God and his love through our example in parenting. This is not a role we can take lightly.

Parenting Priorities

I will be the first to admit that I am a recovering workaholic. I come by it honestly. I come from a long line of workaholics. But we also live in a culture that perpetuates this. In the Western world, most of us are walking around with our stress and productivity levels as a badge of honor. We live in a world that says we need to *earn* our rest and connection with others.

The problem is that, as exiles on this earth, we aren't meant to live by that standard. That distortion is part of what we are called to die to when we decide to live for God. God calls us to a different standard—one where *he* is at the center of everything and, therefore, one where our connection and intention with our kids comes before our jobs, our social lives, our bank accounts, the size of our homes, and our schedules.

God never says we need to earn our rest. Rather, rest is a gift that he commands that we indulge in to get a glimpse into eternity with him.[2] He never says that we need to earn our connection with others—connection is not a luxury that some of us cannot afford. Connection is a *necessity* that we can't afford not to have. Especially with our kids!

As modern-day parents, we must be mindful of our *stated* priorities and our *lived* priorities. Part of our role as godly parents is to prune our lives in such a way that we are able to *wholeheartedly*, while imperfectly, engage the task that God has set before us: to be his representative to our children.

That said, we cannot elevate our role as parents above our role as God's children. In my therapy office, I tend to see two general camps of parents:

(1) parents who are not connecting well with their kids; they are fitting parenting into their lives instead of it being more of a central role and (2) people who have made parenting the most important role in their life; they have idolized the title of "mom" or "dad." The funny thing is that these two types of parents tend to marry each other. And the behavior of one tends to reinforce the counter behavior of the other and round and round they go until they are steeped in conflict.

The answer is somewhere in the *messy middle*. We must look through God's eyes on this and put it into perspective. We are first and foremost *God's*. God's child, God's friend, God's bride, God's beloved. Parenting is an incredibly important task—one that we ought never fit into our lives but devote our whole hearts to. But it's *God* that should be at the center of our parenting. Not Instagram parenting tips, not the expectations of this world, not even our children—God.

Hate Me to Love Me

In my preteen years, I once asked my mom, "What's up with this Luke 14 passage that says you have to hate me in order to love God?" ("If anyone comes to me and does not hate father and mother, wife and children, brothers and sisters—yes, even their own life—such a person cannot be my disciple" [Luke 14:26]). I was borderline offended that my mom would willingly sign up for a way of life in which she was instructed to hate me.

Mom explained to me that she was called to love God so much more than she loved me or anyone else that, in comparison, it looked like hate. My elegant (read: uncouth) response was, "Well, that's stupid! You should just love me as much as you can and love God as much as you can. We'll see who wins!" I was turning my mom's affections into a competition between me and God.

She wisely responded, "Well, Ellen, the more I love God and put him at the center of my life, the more ability I have to love you. You see, God *wants* me to love you, and he wants me to love you well. But I can't love you the way that I'm supposed to unless I love him most."

This is the profound answer I think we are all looking for in godly parenting. Instead of *looking down*, trying to hide from what our kids will encounter in a world outside Eden, or frantically *looking around*, hyper-vigilant in striving to protect our kids from the influences that exist in a post-Edenic world, we need to stop and *look up*. We must continually keep our eyes on God and affix our hearts in heaven above. Then, and *only then*, do we have a shot at loving our kids the way we're called to and being the kind of stewards that God calls us to be in their lives as we navigate this distorted world outside Eden.

 ## Reflect and Discuss

1. What are three things that you have a difficult time surrendering to God as it relates to your child?
2. What parts of your life do you find get in the way of your godly parenting?
3. Describe where you fall on the parenting spectrum—fitting parenting into your life or idolizing parenting.
4. List three changes you can implement today to prioritize godly parenting.

Chapter 2:
Early Childhood (4–6)

I grew up in a Christian home with God at the center of our household. We didn't just go to church on Sundays and Wednesdays. My parents lived out their faith and actively instilled it in their children. As Proverbs 22:6 directs, I was trained in the way that I should go. (Spoiler: I did depart from it when I got older…but I eventually returned.)

In many ways, I had a charmed upbringing. I knew my parents loved me; I was clothed properly; I was adequately fed (perhaps more than adequately); there was lots of laughter and tender care in my upbringing. My parents didn't just love us, they *liked* us too (well, at least most of the time). But, even with all these overwhelming blessings that God instilled in my life and in our family, I still had this festering, gnawing, terrifying insecurity: "You're just like your dad!"

It was meant as a compliment but received as a laceration to my already terrified heart at the tender age of six. You see, my dad fits the traditional cultural stereotype for "masculine." He is tough, in charge, and passionate. My mom is the opposite; she fits the traditional cultural stereotype for "feminine." She is quiet, nurturing, and gentle.

The problem, as I saw it, was that I was more like my dad than I was like my mom. The way my dad and I saw the world, the way we experienced emotion, and the way we expressed ourselves all matched. I desperately studied my mom for similarities between us but I found none, and this devastated me. At a very early age I realized that:

I WAS NOT LIKE MY MOM IN PERSONALITY OR CHARACTER, BUT I WAS LIKE HER IN GENDER.

I WAS NOT LIKE MY DAD IN GENDER, BUT I WAS LIKE HIM IN PERSONALITY AND CHARACTER.

I felt like a riddle gone horribly wrong: "Which one of these is not like the other?" Me!

In my unripe, rudimentary brain, it did not occur to me to talk to my parents about the fear that was constantly smoldering just beneath the surface of my heart. I was not even fully aware of this deep fear. All that I could conceptualize at such a tender age was this: *Something is wrong with me. I'm broken. I'm not a real woman. And it's my fault.*

Gender Typicality

Believe it or not, we start to see signs of sexual orientation development and gender identity awareness as early as the ages of about 4–6 for most children.[3] It's during this developmental stage that children are avid observers of their parents. They start recognizing gender roles within their families and shaping their own expectations regarding gender expression.[4]

Gender typicality forms as children begin to notice whether they behave, think, and process the way that others of their same sex do.[5] The problem is that young brains are unable to grasp any semblance of abstraction or nuance; instead, they cling to concrete, dichotomous "truths." For example, if Dad does the cooking and Mom mows the lawn, children in early childhood can be quick to extrapolate these observations as norms within every family, thus creating rigid beliefs like, "Men cook. Women mow lawns." If they encounter another family that has different household roles, young children may be confused or even judgmental about gender roles that deviate from the norms they see exemplified in their own homes. This judgement may even turn inward and evolve into shame as children become more self-aware and increasingly compare themselves to others of their same sex (see "Gender Contentedness" below).

Speak plainly and confidently to your young children about any discrepancies in gender roles they may observe. Don't wait for your child to bring these observations up to you. Instead, preemptively talk to your kids about *God's* expectations of men and women, thus refuting the gender stereotypes that the world has created. Use stories from the Bible of men and women that break modern cultural norms and instead exemplify the full spectrum of masculinity and femininity.

> **Example:** How was Jesus mighty, courageous, and strong? How was he soft, loving, and nurturing?

Do not pigeonhole personality traits by assigning them to "masculine" or "feminine," but actively praise traits in your child and in others that directly correlate with the nature of God. Avoid stereotypical quips, like "Be tough like a man" or "He throws like a girl." If your child notices a discrepancy in gender roles in a different family, let them hear you affirm other families that have different gender norms.

> **Example:** When you went to Bryce's house, you noticed that his mom mowed the lawn while his dad cooked dinner. That might have seemed odd to you because in our home it's the opposite—your mom usually cooks, and your dad usually mows the lawn.
>
> The truth is that both ways of doing things are good and normal. In some families, the dad prefers to cook, and in some families, the mom prefers to mow the lawn. God made everyone with different talents and

abilities. He is glorified when we use the different talents that he gave us, especially when it's to meet the needs of other people!

It's so great that Bryce's mommy and daddy are each using their abilities and interests to serve their family. Just because people do things differently from the way our family does them doesn't mean it's wrong. In fact, we can always learn from people who do things differently than we do!

Gender Contentedness

Once children become aware of gender norms within their homes and the culture at large, they begin to form personal beliefs about the cultural expectations and stereotypes related to gender.[6] If a child is unable to emulate their personal expectation of gender roles, it may affect their *gender contentedness*, their feeling of efficacy as it relates to their gender.[7]

If Dad is aggressive and unemotional, and little Johnny is highly emotional, artistic, and shy, this could severely impact Johnny's perspective of what is considered "typical" for his gender (*gender typicality*) and thus could negatively impact how content Johnny feels as a male (*gender contentedness*). These kinds of early observations for young children have the potential to lead to a lot of confusion, frustration, and even shame, as a distorted perception can begin to form: "*Something is wrong with me because I'm not like others of my same sex.*" This core distortion often intensifies and proliferates into other distortions as children grow, mainly around their sexuality and gender identity.[8]

If you're the parent of a child in this age range, it's important for you to talk to your child about the body, about sex, and about gender roles (don't worry, we will talk more about how to do that in Chapters 7, 8, and 11). Teach your children what makes men's and women's bodies the same and what makes them different. Normalize these topics and normalize breaking gender stereotypes that the world has constructed. Your daughter needs to know that if she hates dresses and loves monster trucks, she's still a girl because God made her that way; if your son hates sports and likes to bake, he's still a boy because God made him that way.

If you observe a notable contrast in the way your child's same-sex parent expresses their masculinity or femininity compared to your child's, approach the topic with them in a straightforward and simple manner. Use this as an opportunity to teach your child about the nature of God and how each of you images God in a unique way.

> **Example:** Simone, you are very different from Mommy even though we are both girls. That's totally normal! God made you to be like him in very specific ways, and he created Mommy to be like him in specific ways too. We each have different characteristics of God, but we were both equally made in his image! Sometimes we might feel like something is wrong with us because we feel that we don't dress, think, or act like some other girls we know, but the truth is our bodies are what make us alike. All girls don't like to do the same activities or like to act or dress in the same way, and that's okay!

Because You're Mine

When I was growing up, I observed things that were true in my family, but not necessarily true overall. For example, I witnessed my dad become very emotional very quickly, at unexpected moments. Usually, his emotions came out as anger. My mom, on the other hand, rarely expressed any big emotions, least of all anger. These observations led me to the concrete (and faulty) belief that all men are emotional, unpredictable, and angry, while all women are calm, steady, and subdued. This early childhood belief subconsciously followed me throughout my development. Later in life, I realized that I, like my dad, had a deep well of emotion that came out as anger often and unexpectedly and that I was frequently incapable of being calm, levelheaded, and subdued. I assumed this was not just an anger problem; I took it as proof that something was broken in my femininity. In me. "I'm an impostor everywhere I go" became my secret shame.

Similarly, a client, Omar, recalls the loneliness he felt growing up, as he and his dad expressed masculinity differently. These observations shaped a core belief for Omar: "I'm not enough as I am; I must hide my true self in order to gain love and approval from my parents." This distorted belief has influenced every significant relationship in his life, from employers and friends to his spouse and children. Now, in his mid-forties, Omar is having an identity crisis. He wrestles with fatigue from upholding his false persona, a sense of isolation due to the lack of authentic connections, and persistent feelings of inadequacy. He's acutely aware that the affection he has received from his closest relationships has been filtered through the pseudo-self he created in his early years to secure a sense of love and approval.

Because we live in a fallen world, our understanding of God, his love, and our own selves has been fundamentally altered, thus detaching our sense of identity and our worth from its original Source. Our sense of self and value are now formed within this fallen world instead of being anchored to God's perfect love. Each human has to contend with this reality, and we each choose to do it in different ways. Many of us construct pseudo-selves to mask our self-perceived undesirable parts in a bid to secure even a fraction of the love and affection we so deeply yearn for. However, just like quenching thirst with seawater, this false persona merely exacerbates our anxieties, as we recognize that the love and affection we receive is contingent on an artificial self-image. The haunting inner refrain, "If they knew the *real* me, they wouldn't love me," becomes our destructive internal chant, trapping us in a false identity, consumed by the fear of relinquishing the shred of pseudo-worth we are desperately clinging to.[9]

Parents of children in early childhood (and every other stage of development) ought to help their child construct their true self-worth—the one that is wrapped up in Christ with God. God exemplifies unconditional love for us, his children. Though we will imperfectly represent unconditional love to our children, we must do our best to separate our love, affection, and acceptance of them from their traits—even their positive ones.

I recently started asking my kids, "Why do you think I love you?" They would answer with things like, "Because you think I'm cute!" or "I'm good at hugs!"

I would reply, "Well, you are really cute. And you are very good at giving hugs. I love those things about you. But that's not why I love *you*. I love you *because you're mine.*"

Isn't this the message of God's love for us? There's no logical justification for God's love toward us, no apparent advantage to him. He can extend such remarkable, boundless love because it isn't contingent on our qualities, characteristics, or even our obedience to him. His love is solely founded on his guardianship of us, his children. He loves us, not because of who we are or what we do, but because *we are his.* This is the same kind of love we must strive to offer our children to help combat the distorted beliefs that will inevitably assail their sense of identity and worth throughout their development.

 ## Reflect and Discuss

1. What kinds of early observations about gender norms do you remember from your upbringing?
2. What early observations or questions has your child expressed that you have felt ill-equipped to respond to?
3. Describe what life in your home might look like through your child's eyes as it relates to gender norms and gender typicality.
4. What has been your experience with your own pseudo-self and pseudo-worth?

Chapter 3:
Middle Childhood (7–11)

While the emphasis in early childhood (4–6) lies in a child's observations and distorted beliefs, the emphasis shifts in middle childhood (7–11) to social competence and education. Early childhood is a sweet, nostalgic stage when parents make up a child's whole world, but in middle childhood, their narrow sphere of influence expands to include peers. Parents are still a major influence in their child's life, but now there is an ever-growing competition for influence: friends!

Social Competence

A key component in this stage of development is *social competence*,[10] or the ability to create and maintain meaningful relationships. Social competence is the lubricant to our connection with others. It aids in building self-esteem, communication skills, identity, and overall cultural fluency.

Struggling with aspects of social competence can be disastrous enough for children. But if a lack of social competence is coupled with unresolved issues from the previous stage of development, mainly gender contentedness (how content a person feels in their gender), this could really snowball for a child and create some difficulties. Most notably, they could have a difficult time relating to peers of the same gender. If prolonged, this could create or reinforce an already existing distorted belief that they do not belong within their assigned gender. The belief that they do not belong in their God-given gender can complicate a child's understanding of their own gender identity or sexual attraction.

Parents of children in this age range ought to aid them in their peer connection. Our kids need to be able to grow in their confidence with connecting to their peers. A great way to help your children learn these practical skills is to practice them during your family devotionals (see Chapter 5). Have your child pretend to be on the playground and approach a "peer" (you) and ask them to play. Or have them practice how to respond to questions and then ask a question in return, "I had a good weekend, thanks for asking. What did you do this weekend?"

I remember one such family devotional when I was growing up when my parents taught one of my younger brothers how to look someone in the eye when they were speaking. They then taught me how to smile when listening to someone, instead of giving full reign to my natural, resting scowl. Especially in such a technological world where these social skills are ebbing among our youth, our children need us to make sure that we are giving them plenty of opportunities to learn, practice, and implement these skills.

Education

The central focus in middle childhood is *education*. This is a much more expansive definition of education than the type of education kids receive in schools. The kind of developmental education kids receive in this stage teaches them what their culture values and what the measure of success is in their society.

Although we want to be the primary educators in our kids' lives, the truth is, this type of education happens everywhere, all the time! In our homes, our churches, on TV, on social media, in peer relationships, in public—everywhere we look, we find major clues as to what our culture deems important. Think about the kinds of lessons kids are learning in our culture right now:

- ❖ Your emotion = truth.
- ❖ If someone disagrees with you, they hate you; if you disagree with someone, you hate them.
- ❖ Love of self is the most important type of love.
- ❖ Being in a majority is inherently bad; being in a minority is inherently good.

These faulty earthly ideologies are visible everywhere in our culture, and our kids are soaking them all up like sponges during their most formative years. These twisted truths are absolutely affecting our children's gender and sexual identities. Most children in middle childhood, even those growing up in Christian homes, would not even be able to perceive that homosexuality and crossing gender boundaries is not what God wants for his people.

If you are the parent of a child in this age range, it will be helpful to utilize part of your family time together to discuss some of the things that your children are observing and learning in our culture. Be sure to allow your child space to share any emotions, questions, or thoughts about what they are seeing and hearing; then seek to put God at the middle of it all, balancing out God's nature by representing the messy middle—striving to uphold both unconditional love and unwavering righteousness equally. Don't wait for your child to bring some of these things up. Sometimes parents need to be the initiator.

> **Example:** You saw two men kissing today. That must have been very confusing for you since you have never seen that before. Was there anything else you thought or felt about seeing that?

The truth is that's common in our world today. Some men are dating or married to other men, and some women are dating or married to other women. This is not what God wants for his people, but God allows us to make these kinds of decisions for ourselves.

In this family, we believe that romantic relationships, which includes kissing, should just be between a man and a woman, since that's how God created us to exist. However, we do not look down on, judge, or disrespect anyone that doesn't agree with us or lives a different way.

It's okay to have different beliefs than other people, and it's okay for people to live differently than we do. The most important thing to be aware of is that God loves them and calls us to *love them too*.

It's important to note that it's both expected and perfectly acceptable that you will not always have the exact right answers for your children. What matters most is that they feel secure in their connection with you and are comfortable approaching you about what they are seeing and learning in our culture. Your aim is not to always be right, but to be a dependable source of unconditional love and guidance—continually building a deep bond and safety between you and your child.

Boundaries

Middle childhood is a great time to implement stricter boundaries for our kids. Boundaries are tough for a lot of us because we tend to either see them as unloving, and therefore we don't have many boundaries; or our boundaries are too strict because they stem from fear and not love. But neither one of these approaches will serve our children well. If there were one thing I really want to scare Christian parents about, it would be the dangers of neglecting good, healthy, God-centered boundaries with your kids.

Psalm 23:4 says, "Your rod and your staff, they comfort me." A rod and staff were instruments of discipline—of boundary—between a shepherd and a sheep. Boundaries are meant to protect us and provide safety for us and our children. It's a parent's job to implement boundaries, it's a child's job to push against them—we can just expect that. We don't need to get angry about it, that's how they learn. And *how* we uphold our boundaries affects *what* they learn—whether it's a boundary they will internalize or not.

We, as God's people, hold to his unchanging, immovable hand as he sets boundaries for us. Boundaries comfort us because we know what to expect and that God's love will not change, whether we abide by them or not. We, as godly parents, need to exude the same kind of steadfastness with our kids—both in our love and in our boundaries for them.

God doesn't decide on boundaries for us based on what's best for him or based on how he thinks we might react to them. Rather, he creates boundaries based on what's best for *us*. We need to imitate our heavenly Parent's motivation and execution in our own boundary-making with our children. Here are a few things to consider as you are making boundaries for your children:

- ❖ What will my (the parent's) personal conscience allow?
- ❖ What is in the best interest of my family overall?
- ❖ What is in the best interest of my child (trying to balance what is best physically, emotionally, mentally, and spiritually)?

Things that we may be aware of, but do not want to let dictate our boundaries for our kids are things like:

- ❖ How will my child react?
- ❖ How will others perceive me?
- ❖ What is the quickest and easiest way to go about this?

We all will have to stand before the Lord one day, and we will want to pledge a clear conscience about the way that we stewarded our children's hearts toward him. And "I didn't want to deal with their tantrum," or "None of my friends were implementing that boundary for their kids" will not be sufficient arguments. Just like with the parable of the talents,[11] our Master will one day hold us accountable for whether we have been faithful, diligent, and sacrificial in what he has entrusted us with—the hearts of our children.[i]

Whenever I talk with parents about boundaries, I'm always asked, "What boundaries should we set with our kids?" Unfortunately, there are no quick, easy universal boundaries that ought to be applied to every child in every family. Boundaries often depend on your personal conscience, your family culture, and your child's maturity level. However, here are some areas to consider as you're implementing boundaries in your home in this stage:

Time Spent Together as a Family. In my home growing up, my parents were working in ministry and were very busy in the evenings. But they had a rule that we would eat dinner together as a family at least four evenings during the week and that we would have a family devotional together at least once per week. This saved us from being swept up into the culture of busyness that we found ourselves surrounded by.

Time Spent with Others. Though we want to ensure that our children are getting ample social time with peers, we also want to help them develop a healthy balance in their social influences. Talk to your kids about how we are influenced by others' character (1 Corinthians 15:33) and how to develop healthy same-sex friendships (see Appendix 2: FAQs—Parenting Through the Developmental Stages).

Access to Electronics and Social Media. I find that a lot of modern-day parents are shockingly unconcerned about their children's electronic/social media access until it's too late. But this is the time to be mind-

---

i   I am not referring to outcomes here. I am simply talking about our own dedication and heart in stewarding our children, regardless of the outcome. The journey of faith is complex, influenced by many factors beyond a parent's control.

ful of boundaries in these areas, when your kids are younger, before they are inundated with too many concepts that they are unable to process.

My husband and I started talking about boundaries around electronics and media influence when I was pregnant with our first child. For example, we decided that we did not want our kids as teenagers to have access to any electronics in their rooms, behind closed doors. Instead, iPads, computers, and phones would have to be used in the common areas of the house where there was more oversight. Because we thought through these boundaries early in our children's lives, we were able to implement that boundary when they were young, so that our kids never got used to having electronics in their rooms and didn't face having that taken away when they got older. We're not looking to punish them; we are looking to protect them.

It is never too early to contextualize boundaries (present or future) and even begin implementing them now, before they are desperately needed. Of course, as our kids get older, we'll need to renegotiate these boundaries and make them age appropriate to suit their ever-growing autonomy, but we want, as much as possible, to implement them ahead of time in a way that sets the kind of safety that the rod and staff in Psalm 23 portrays.

 ## Reflect and Discuss

1. What are your fears regarding what your child is learning in our current culture?
2. What do you remember about your social competence and peer relationships while growing up?
3. What difficulties has your child had with social competence and peer interactions?
4. How do you think technology is affecting your child?

Chapter 4:

Early Adolescence (12–18)

Proverbs 22:6 provides encouragement to parents—if we train our children in the way they ought to go when they're young, there is hope that they will stay on the path when they are older.[ii] The chaos that bridges guiding our children down a godly path and them continuing down it when they're older is known as early adolescence. The preteen and teenage years are not an easy time for children or parents. But I hate to be the one that breaks it to you—it's normal. In fact, it's good. It's even God-ordained!

This is the stage of life that God created for children to begin to push away from their parents.[12] This is a biological function that every species needs in order to survive. If we remain dependent on our parents our whole lives, we will die out as a human race.[13] Therefore, God created a

---

ii   Some parents find Proverbs 22:6 anything *but* encouraging. They worry that, if our child does depart from the path we set, never to return, we are to blame. But the Bible does not guarantee specific outcomes for our children's faith based on our parenting practices. Our parenting is just one aspect of our children's journey of faith, character, and personality development, and not the sole determining factor.

function in children's brains, right around the preteen and teenage years, that helps to facilitate this necessary separation that allows our children to assert their own identity, values, beliefs, and morals. This is good! Not only is separation needed biologically to survive, but it is also essential for spiritual survival.

Our children cannot ride the coattails of our faith forever. The kind of faith we hope our children will develop cannot survive unless they go through this separation process. It's scary to watch our children begin this separation at a time when their brains are still being formed, but that's why they need us to come alongside them and help them through it.

From Strict Boundaries to Soft Bumpers

Recall what it was like when your child first started walking. It might have been a bit scary, or maybe even sad for you to watch them enter this new developmental stage. But ultimately you knew that it was good and right, and you helped them through it. You probably even took them by the hands and guided them through the process. We want to employ the same measures with our kids in their preteen and teenage years as they gradually toddle their way into autonomy. Just as you probably covered the fireplace with padded cushioning or put child locks on the cabinets when your child first started walking, we want to set up healthy boundaries for our preteens and teenagers so that they have cushioned falls from their unsteady steps as they learn to take over some of these executive functions on their own.

This is the time to shift from teaching our children *what* to think and instead teach them *how* to think. Our parenting role in the teenage years slowly morphs into something akin to serving as bowling bumpers: We provide guidance and boundaries for our kids while they wobble and determine which direction they will go, but they are beginning to make some of those choices for themselves *within the limits we have set.*

I distinctly remember one such transition in my own life. I was about fifteen years old, and I had a soccer game. I planned on going to my game until my friends invited me to a social event that was much more interesting to me. I asked my parents if I could skip my game. They offered me three possible responses, but only two were options I was allowed to choose from:

1. **The Godly Response:** Miss the social engagement and go to the game because you made a commitment, and your team is depending on you.

2. **The Integrity Response:** Call your coach and tell him the truth about why you will not be coming to the game and apologize for going back on your commitment.

3. **The Worldly Response:** Miss the game without informing the coach OR lie to the coach as to the reason you could not attend. (My parents made it abundantly clear that this was not an option for me.)

This parenting formula became a common "bumper" for my brother and me in our teenage years together. Our parents gave us more and more autonomy and decision-making ability over our lives, but it still had its limits. And crossing those limits had consequences.

Our children's autonomy is not a light switch. It's more like a dimmer switch. We slowly increase the level of freedom and autonomy that our children have as they mature, providing bumpers along the way to continue to train them in the way they ought to go when they are older.

The Teenage Brain

Was there ever a scarier and more complicated topic than the teenage brain? I bet it would be very difficult to find an adult who would willingly go back in time to their teenage years—and for good reason! This is a complicated and often chaotic and confusing time of life, in part because the brain is undergoing a major remodel from the ages of about twelve to twenty-four.[14]

The part of the brain that is very well formed in this stage is the *primitive brain*, which is responsible for basic human needs that keep us alive— things like breathing and blinking. The primitive brain is also responsible for the creation of emotions, like anger and fear.[15] This part of our brain is incredibly important and has kept our species alive for millions of years!

The part of the teenage brain that is not fully developed during this stage is the *frontal lobe*. The frontal lobe is responsible for the regulation of emotions. This is also the part of the brain that plans ahead and weighs the risks of certain behaviors.[16] It can be quite uncomfortable for parents to witness the discrepancy here—one minute, their teenager is speaking with a maturity far beyond their years, and the next minute they are erupting into a tantrum that transports parents back to the toddler years.

As parents, navigating our teens' fluctuations can be frustrating and confusing. But if you think this is a confusing time for you, *imagine how confusing it is for your teenager*! Being sensitive to teens' confusion may help you to have some empathy and compassion for what your child is going through. Let them hear you say, "Wow, that is so tough. I can't even imagine," as they describe their experiences to you.

The best thing we can do for our children as their brains are developing is to help them develop an integrated brain.[17] And we can do this by helping them to expand the lens of their emotional experiences. We can calmly and lovingly help our children discern (1) what they are feeling and (2) why they are feeling that way; and then we can help them to (3) rationalize what the best response is or what the God-centered perspective is.

We should be careful to never shame our teenagers for their incomplete brains. It's not their fault! Instead, we must normalize their need for growth and give them hope that their emotional swings will not be their reality forever. We need to not only understand the teenage brain ourselves, as parents, but we must also help our children understand the incapacities of their own developing brains and the dangers of making lifelong decisions that may not correlate with their lifelong desires.

My dad used to do this for me when I was a teenager by telling me on multiple occasions, "It'll make more sense when you have matured a bit." He wasn't placing a judgement on me or speaking with a condescending tone; he said it in the same way that he used to say, "One day you'll be tall enough to reach that cupboard on your own." Dad was making a matter-of-fact statement that allowed me to recognize that my brain was not yet fully formed—a fact I had no direct control over. This encouragement from my dad brought me no shame. It helped me look forward to the day I would have a fully formed brain and would be able to understand things in a new and different way.

Identity

Another important thing that's happening for our kids during this stage is their search for where they belong in this world outside our homes—they are looking for *group identity*.[18] This is part of the separation process. Preteens and teens need to develop connections besides those that already exist within their family of origin. We don't have to be threatened by that as parents; in fact, we can aid them in this process by encouraging healthy connections outside our homes. We can also implement bumpers around these connections to ensure that they are not spending too much time with any one friend or group of friends.

Healthy group identity is similar to a healthy diet—balance is key. Broccoli is healthy, yes? But eating only broccoli could be extremely unhealthy. Similarly, we want to put some bumpers around our children's time with friends to help our kids have multiple areas of connection and identity, ensuring a healthy, balanced "identity diet."

Finding an identity during this age range is important and can feel scary and all-consuming for children. We need to continue to build intentional connection with our children within our homes to persistently fuel that part of their identity. But most importantly, we need to remind them that God has already given our child a robust identity in him. It doesn't even have to be curated—the work is already done! It's our job to continually point our kids to the mirror of God's eyes, reminding them of who they really are—God's son or daughter—fully and unconditionally beloved by the Creator of the cosmos.

When my husband and I were first married, I spoke very rudely to him as we were hanging out with some friends. One of our friends stopped me and said, "Ellen, do you realize who you're talking to right now? That's not just your husband whom you can speak to however you'd like. *That's God's son.*" A shiver went down my spine. We must be committed to looking at our children through the same lens—God's beloved children whom he has uniquely entrusted us with. We can't just *tell* our kids that they have an active identity in Christ, we must *treat* them like it too.

 ## Reflect and Discuss

1. What has the separation process looked like for you and your child?
2. Are boundaries easy or difficult for you to implement? Why?
3. What do you remember about your own identity search as a teenager? What kinds of things formed your identity at the time?
4. What do you see your child heavily identifying with in their own search for identity, meaning, and purpose?

PART 2

Laying the Groundwork: Creating the Foundation for LGBTQ+ Conversations

E ncountering matters of sex, sexuality, and gender can be difficult enough when it is just us as individuals standing before God. When our kids get added to that equation, the fear, grief, and discomfort tend to amplify exponentially. Now that we have an understanding of what is happening with our children developmentally, we are ready to contextualize the LGBTQ+ conversation for them. This section will offer practical guidance as you build the foundation for creating the space and the frame of heart needed to educate your kids about sex, sexuality, gender, and LGBTQ+ topics.

Chapter 5:

Intentional Connection

Intentional connection is my clinical way of trying to depict what family devotionals looked like for me growing up. When I was a kid, we had devotionals on a weekly basis. These are some of the fondest memories I have from childhood. Here I often felt the most seen, heard, understood, nurtured, and connected with my family, and this carried me throughout the week.

Looking back, I'm able to see all the intangibles, the unseen things, that were happening in my developing heart during these family times. To feel as if you belong is an innate need in all of us, especially in our formative years. These times of connection created a sense of belonging for me within my family to which I tethered my core identity, even as I got older and started to piece together my identity with aspects of life outside my parent's home.

These times also created a tremendous amount of safety for me. They conveyed to me that I was important and worthy enough for my parents to take time out of their lives each week to focus on actively connecting with and training my brother and me. They also created a safe space to discuss a lot of necessary topics that every child should talk through with their parents, like LGBTQ+ topics.

I remember my parents using one such devotional to teach my brother and me how to respond if a stranger offered an incentive to get into their car. They used another devotional to teach us how to discern appropriate from inappropriate touch from others. In my preteen years, when I was assailed by pubescent hormones, my parents taught me how to control my tone of voice when I had big emotions, and they taught me the difference a smile makes in conversation. Vulnerable discussion and teaching within our family allowed me to feel safe enough to ask questions that sometimes felt difficult and embarrassing for me as a child, like, "What does 'gay' mean?"

The first thing parents need to do in teaching their kids about sex, sexuality, gender, and LGBTQ+ topics is to create the space to discuss such tender topics. The second thing that is needed for having these delicate conversations is a deep sense of safety and connection between parent and child. Family devotionals can provide both for your family.

Intention Yields Quality

I prefer *intentional* in describing family devotionals because it really is the key to making these times great. I could spend three hours sitting next to my child, each of us wrapped up in our own thoughts and activities. We would probably both walk away from this time feeling less connected than before. Time is important, yes, but it is the *intention* behind the time that shifts the measure of time from quantity to quality. It is the quality of the time spent with our loved ones that makes a difference, and *that* requires intention. Family devotionals can serve as concentrated quality time.

Whenever I talk to clients about having family devotionals or creating intentional times of connection with their kids on a weekly basis, I always feel the proverbial eye roll happening inside them. I get it. It's hard, life is busy, sometimes our kids aren't into it. It's hard to start new patterns in our families—there really are a million reasons *not* to implement these times of intentional connection within our families.

But almost every parent that I've spoken to who did not stick with family devotionals when their children were young has regretted not building that framework from an early age. Instead, these parents are having to retroactively dismantle unhealthy connection habits their family has formed and rebuild healthy connection habits. This is a lot harder to do after the fact. Family devotionals are an investment in the safety, sense of belonging, and godly lens that we hope to cultivate in our children's hearts. We may not see the benefits immediately, but it will have a big return later.

If you are reading this and you have not maintained regular times of connection with your kids in their early years, that's okay! *It's never too late to start.*

Each family's approach to devotionals will be distinct. There is no one-size-fits-all formula for devos. Utilize the remainder of this chapter as a foundation for tailoring your family devotionals to align with your family's unique structure and needs. For instance, if you are a single parent and family devos every week feels too taxing for you to plan, consider inviting other families to participate in your devotionals, taking turns educating the children about spiritual concepts and stories. If you are the only Christian in your household, you could opt for "family meetings," rather than centering the time on God. If you have a child with a neurodevelopmental disorder for whom sitting and talking for longer periods are difficult, consider scheduling intentional discussions during certain drive times throughout the week. The primary objective of family devotionals is to foster connection and revel in your one-of-a-kind family culture and dynamic—no matter when, where, or how that connection happens.

Components of a Family Devotional

Establishing family devotionals can feel new, different, and uncomfortable. Here are some guidelines that your family can follow to make this an enjoyable and fruitful time together.

Establish a regular schedule. Creating a set date, time, and space for family devotionals can not only provide safety in routine, but it also allows you and your children to subconsciously be preparing your hearts throughout the day or week to revel in your family connection during your devo. It also gives parents a dedicated time to have difficult discussions with their children. "We'll talk about it at our next family devo" was a common response from my parents when faced with a request from one of their children in the middle of the week. Having this set time prevented my parents from having to respond to behavioral issues or cultural influences in the heat of the moment, when emotions were usually high. Instead, they were afforded time to think, pray, and process our requests or influences before our next family devotional when we were all more emotionally regulated.

Make devotional times distraction-free. These important times of family connection should not happen with the TV on or while your kids finish their homework. These family devotionals ought to be concentrated times of connection with no distractions present. There should be plenty of times when you spend time together as a family while simultaneously doing other things—and these times are important and special too! But family devotionals are an activity all on their own. No distractions can serve as a relief during this sacred time of purposeful bonding.

Keep them fun. Devotional times together as a family were so much fun for my brother and me because my parents were clearly enjoying themselves and not just putting on a show for us. We had authentic fun together, my parents included. They did not want these times to feel like rote, obligatory family meetings. They were a time for us to revel in our family culture, in our connection, and in our love for one another. There is no better way to do this than to have fun together!

Sometimes we played a game before our time of devotion, or watched a movie after our devotional, or went on a hike and had our devotional out in the wilderness. One time we all wrote down different fun activities that we wanted to do together on little pieces of paper: go bowling, go out to eat, see a movie, go ice skating, etc. We folded up our respective ideas and put them into a hat, then took turns each week drawing out one of the fun activities to do together after our family devotional. These are some of my most cherished memories of fun from my childhood.

Take time to worship. We were no von Trapp Family Singers, but we did enjoy worshiping God through prayer and song together as a family. This was not usually a somber worship of God. It was a fun, raucous, joyful worship of the Lord.

We would all eye my dad during the chorus of one particular song where he always mixed up the words. My brother would perform a solo, making his voice too deep and gravely for a boy of six (a tradition his children have continued to this day). We would laugh and laugh, wordlessly building the distinctions of our family culture and silently sewing in lifelong memories of connection that bonded us together in unseen ways.

What helped us as children to get into the singing and enjoy it was seeing that my parents' hearts were clearly into it. They practiced what they preached on this! If they told us to sing loudly, they were singing three times as loudly and as energetically to set the tone and example for us to follow.

Incorporate education about God. Because God was at the center of my parents' lives, he was also at the center of our home and our connection. It was important to my parents that our family devotionals focus on God. Sometimes these educational moments about God involved learning from important stories in the Bible, like when we read and subsequently acted out Noah packing up the ark.

My parents marched our stuffed animals up the plank of our makeshift ark while I mimicked a doubtful neighbor making fun of Noah for his doomsday prep as the bright sun shone. Later, my little brother played the regretful neighbor that held onto the "ark" (the coffee table) while begging to be let in as the "floods" (my mom dousing us with water from a spray bottle) crashed in.

But these God-centered times were not always based on a famous story from the Bible. Sometimes my parents directly dealt with something that was happening in our lives and strove to put God at the center of it.

I remember one devotional, after a heavy week of arguing between my brother and me, when we repeated Ephesians 4:3, "Make every effort to keep the unity of the Spirit through the bond of peace," over and over. We discussed how this pertained to our sibling relationship, then we went through real-life scenarios where our unity might be threatened and talked about what efforts we might employ to preserve it.

As we got into our teenage years and our interest in God waned for a time, discussions became a bit more abstract as my parents tried to teach us fundamental godly concepts without always directly bringing him to the center of the conversation (e.g., "integrity" instead of "righteousness"). Though my parents never hid their affection for and devotion to God and regularly brought him up to us, they kept a balance in our teen years by not exasperating us with a constant barrage of God-centered conversation. This showed us four important things:

1. Our lack of devotion to God did not shake my parents' faith.
2. They were not afraid to continue talking to us about God, even if our response was huffing and eye rolls.
3. They respected our age-appropriate freedoms and gave us more and more autonomy to choose what we believed as we matured.
4. Their love for us did not depend on our love for God.

Our family devotionals and times of connection and fun together continued, even when my brother and I did not want them to be centered on God. My parents still found a way to sew the tenets of their faith into our hearts, sometimes without always explicitly mentioning the Lord.

We do this all the time as exiles on this earth, don't we? I do it with clients that don't have a faith base. Instead of quoting Proverbs 15:1, "A gentle answer turns away wrath, but a harsh word stirs up anger," I talk to a client about primary and secondary emotional responses and deescalating strategies. It's the same God-created principle, just expressed in a way that does not put God at the center of it. If we are God's creation, and his principles are the manual for how to live the best life we can on this earth, the best thing we can offer to our children is to teach them these principles, even if they are not interested in the Author of them.

I have clients who have implemented intentional times of connection with their teenagers and just call them family meetings, or the "weekly state of the family union." If God cannot be at the center of this time together as a family, that's okay! It's still worth implementing this special time to create connection between you and your kids.

Include practical conversation and a time for touching base. These family devotionals served as a time for my brother and me to gain practical knowledge and application for real-life issues. These were the tender moments when we would discuss big, scary topics for our small, developing hearts. Discussions surrounding divorce, sexuality, talking to strangers, alcohol, money management, the dangers of peer influence, and so much more, all happened during family devotionals. It's important to point out that these conversations were not unique to this time together as a family, but because my parents intentionally discussed these difficult concepts with us during our family devotionals, we felt safe approaching them about these topics outside of those times, whenever we really needed their guidance and direction.

A word of caution: You might want to ask questions to make sure you understand what your child's question *actually is*. Because I felt so safe discussing issues openly with my family, at the age of seven, I once asked, "Mom, what is a period?"

She stopped what she was doing, calmly came over to me, took a deep breath, and explained menses to me. When she was done, she said, "Where did you hear that term?"

I said, "On a TV show; someone said they skipped first period at school." She then had to backtrack and explain to me the *other* kind of period, a measure of time in a school environment. The moral of the story is: Perhaps get the context of what your child is *really* asking, lest you explain too much!

Taking Advantage of Spontaneous Connection

Connection with our kids does not just happen once a week; it should happen continually and in different ways throughout the week. I once had a client who wanted help with building a deeper connection with her kids. She was baffled at the lack of cohesion within their family. When I asked her what their dinners looked like she said, "Well, I make dinner and we all go off to our own respective corners of the house and eat on our own." One important place that family connection and communication happen is at the dinner table. When I was young, we used to do an exercise during dinner, "highs and lows," when we each shared one best thing and one worst thing about our day. This was a great way to aid in our daily connection as a family.

Family devotionals can exist as one type of intentional connection, but we have lots of other opportunities in life to utilize times of connection. I remember car rides being a great time to have meaningful conversation; both as a family, and individually with one of my parents. Sometimes my mom would be able to break through my hardened, teenage exterior more effectively in one fifteen-minute car ride than in a whole week of sit-down discussions. My dad figured out that my brother would open up if his hands were busy, so they would often build model airplanes together while Dad artfully drew out the depths of my brother's heart. Become a perpetual student of your child(ren) and find out when and where they feel safest to let their guard down and connect so that you can have both intentional and spontaneous moments of connection within your family.

Once deep connection, both intentional and spontaneous, are fixtures in your family, you have the space and relationship necessary to teach your children about the core aspects of God that they need to know in order to understand sex, sexuality, gender, and LGBTQ+ topics from a biblical perspective.

Reflect and Discuss

1. What are the biggest barriers to maintaining connection within your family?
2. What are your thoughts, hopes, and fears about family devotionals?
3. What kinds of practical life advice do you think would be beneficial to your children during family devotionals?

Chapter 6:

Rave, Rant, Repent (and Revel!)

When I was about six years old, my dad heard of this concept from a guest speaker that came to teach at our church. It was called, "Rave, Rant, and Repent." This forever changed the trajectory of our family connection and communication as we implemented this framework into our family devotionals. Here's how it works:

Rave: a praise to offer someone in the family
Rant: a grievance to air to someone in the family
Repent: an area of growth for you to humbly admit to the family

Rave

When we sat down for a family devotional, my parents were very intentional about actively calling out our good deeds or positive character traits displayed in the previous week. They would nitpick in the best way and get specific and detailed about what we did that they were impressed with or proud of.

> **Example:** Ellen, I saw that during the church event there was a little girl not playing with the rest of the kids and you went over and talked to her. We are so proud of you! You have an amazing ability to notice those on the outskirts and pull them in to be included, just like Jesus!

> **Example:** Stephen, you had a conversation with a neighbor today and looked them in the eye the whole time! And after they asked you how your day was, you reciprocated by asking them how their day was! We know this has been hard for you, but you did it! You were polite and delightful as you carried on a conversation with someone, even when you may not have wanted to. You have such an amazing ability to adapt and persevere. We are so proud of you!

These kinds of deep, descriptive praises helped to breed many things in our hearts. What a lesson this was for me in God's attentiveness and delight! I felt seen, heard, and understood—not alone and not forgotten, like so many children often feel. I felt like there was an incentive to do good because it pleased my parents. I knew that it pleased them because they took the time and effort to *recognize it* and then *express it*.

Tears instantly spring to my eyes whenever I reflect on the name that Hagar gave God, *El Roi*, "The God Who Sees."[19] Doesn't this speak to the deepest desire of all our hearts? To be fully seen and known by another? This, after all, is the foundation of intimacy—to know and be fully known. If you want to have deep intimacy with your children, you must *see* them. Observe them throughout the week, then express your gratitude and admiration for them with specific and intentional raves. This takes effort! We must train our brains to be alert for the positives. Be on the lookout for what you can praise your kids for! Ask yourself questions at the end of each day to help draw these into your sphere of awareness. Questions like, "When did I feel most proud of my children today?" "What did they do that was difficult for them today?" "In what ways did my child image God today?"

My parents encouraged my brother and me to express raves for each other or for them by helping to draw them out of our hearts with questions like, "What did your sibling, mom, or dad do this week that made you proud of them?" "That made you feel safe?" "That made you feel loved?" We were encouraged to really think through the week. There was never a rave too small! Every piece of praise was savored and valued.

Rant

Once we finished the raves, there was an opportunity for anyone to share a rant with someone else. No one had to have a rant, but the rule was that, if someone did have one, they had to have a rave to follow it up. Rants were not meant to be a mic-drop moment when we got to tear someone apart for their thoughtless action or comment. This was a time to vulnerably expose the *pain* that someone else caused at any point during the week to inform them of the ripple effect of their action that they might have been unaware of.

> **Example:** (From my brother) Ellen, on Monday you had a friend over, and you didn't let me play with you guys. That made me angry. (After prompts from my parents to pull out the primary emotion under the anger) It made me sad, and I felt left out.

Once a rant was shared, the other person had a chance to respond to it with an apology and further explanation as to their intent.

> **Example:** I'm really sorry that we hurt your feelings. That was not what we were trying to do. We were

talking about stuff that would have been uncomfortable if you were there. That's why we didn't let you play with us. What if next time we set a time limit? We could say, "For the next ten minutes we will play just us, and then we will all play together."

By the way, there is no way we could have been that concise and thoughtful in our communication at such a young age, but the gist of that response eventually came after several prompts, intercessions, and nudges from our parents to help us to (1) recognize the depth of our hearts, (2) communicate it to one another, and (3) come to a resolution together.

One of the best things about incorporating our rants into our weekly scheduled devotional time was that it freed us up from feeling compelled to express our secondary emotion (usually anger) in a moment of high emotional conflict. There was a set time every week when we could check in with each other and share the good and bad from the week. Eventually, we learned that we didn't need to blow up at each other in the moment. In fact, we realized it was more effective when we waited, calmed ourselves, and found a way to vulnerably express our primary emotion (usually hurt) during a rant.

Repent

Once rants were expressed, we had a time to share any "repents" that we needed to unburden from our hearts. My dad was especially good at modeling for us how to humbly expose our areas of growth without being ashamed. He would often say something like, "I have been feeling really remorseful about losing my temper with you guys earlier this week. I had a tough day at work and was preoccupied in my mind and heart with how I was going to try to fix it the next day. Then you guys started asking me a lot of questions, and I felt overwhelmed and took it out on you. That wasn't okay, and I am really working on finding a better way to communicate in moments like that. Will you forgive me?"

This kind of admission from my dad helped my brother and me to grasp a few important things:

1. It isn't shameful to be imperfect. Even our parents were imperfect, so it was okay for us to be imperfect too.
2. There is always a reason why someone mistreats someone else. However, that reason does not nullify the transgression.
3. When our imperfection hurts someone, it is necessary to *ask* for forgiveness.

Most importantly, this repair attempt from my dad modeled genuine connection and relationship—hurts and all. We cannot avoid hurting those we love, because we are imperfect beings; however, we can learn to make repair attempts quickly and effectively, assuring our children that we are committed to allowing our love to cover over our imperfect parenting.

This portion of the Rave, Rant, Repent model can also serve as a time for us, as parents, to model repentance before God to our children. In fact, this practice is perhaps our most valuable tool in modeling for our children how to walk with the Lord.

One of the most impactful things I ever witnessed in my family growing up happened when I was just seven years old. During our devotional that night, my mom contritely confessed to us that she had lied to her boss that day. She told her boss that she was on her way back from lunch when in fact she was still in a store shopping. Both of my parents shared with us the harm in lying and taught, from the Bible, why God calls us to be truthful even when it hurts. My mom shared her remorse and her plan for repentance.

This was more inspiring and educational than a million illustrations of her righteousness. My mother's authenticity showed me some key truths about God and humanity: (1) It's not shameful to need to repent; no one is perfect,[20] not even my parents. (2) It's okay to not be perfect—that's not our ultimate goal. Our ultimate goal is to *strive* for perfection, knowing we will never fully reach it.[21] (3) We can quickly, humbly, and gratefully accept God's grace when we fall short of perfection.[22] (4) As Christians we should be open about repentance and boast in our weaknesses.[23]

We do not need to hide our brokenness from our children; in fact, we can't. We simply need to be open and repentant in our brokenness. (Of course, age appropriately. We shouldn't be sharing sexual sin with our six-year-olds.) I am moved when I think about the sacrifice and act of love it took for my parents to share this very vulnerable news with their children. They were not interested in showcasing some facade of perfection. They were interested in true discipleship to Jesus—messy as it is. When they sinned, their instinct wasn't to hide; it was to expose their sin in order to continue to steward their hearts and their children's hearts toward God.

How amazing is it that God will allow us to use our brokenness to teach our children about him? Our imperfection is not a hindrance in our parenting; it is a powerful tool! God can use it as a tool to help our children see him fully. Therefore, the best thing we can communicate to our children is not our perfection, but our repentance.

Revel

I have a deep fear of not soaking up every ounce of joy, love, and fun out of life. This fear used to steal my attention during important life moments. I remember standing at the altar thinking, "Be present, Ellen! Don't miss this!" I felt assailed with pre-grief over not being able to bask in that moment forever. Mary's example of storing up, treasuring, and pondering important life moments in her heart[24] has offered me a new course in managing this fear: *to revel.*

Revel is an addendum that my husband, kids, and I have added to the Rave, Rant, Repent model. We go around and discuss the moment(s) from the week that we want to savor, even if the moment we are individually reveling in does not include the other family members. This allows each of us to participate in the important moments in each other's life, even if we were not directly involved.

"I loved eating popcorn while watching the movie," my four-year-old will share. "I had this really unexpected and great time of worship in the car on the way home on Tuesday. I was just singing so loudly, from my heart, to God," my husband will reveal. "I loved when you snuggled up to me while we were reading a book at bedtime," I'll express to my son.

These vulnerable disclosures allow our family members to see what we treasure. They help us to know and understand each other better. They help our family to savor life together and bring each other into these special moments. And they help us highlight these important moments in our own consciousness, thus training our brain to be more aware of these golden life moments throughout our busy days.

Life is made up of these little, treasured moments. Don't miss them! *Revel* in them. Together.

Creating the Connection Necessary for LGBTQ+ Conversations

Through the practice of Rave, Rant, Repent, and Revel you can cultivate an abundance of connection, understanding, and healthy communication that can facilitate LGBTQ+ discussions with your children. Rave, Rant, and Repent creates moments that deposit love, cohesion, safety, and identity into the family bank, thus creating a surplus of connection that can cover over a multitude of transgressions, instances of disconnection, and misperceptions. This surplus is needed as your children gradually mature into autonomy. And this surplus of connection is *desperately* needed to navigate LGBTQ+ discussions. This model also enables your family to strengthen essential emotional and communication skills required for respectful and loving discussions on challenging subjects, including LGBTQ+ topics.

 ## Reflect and Discuss

1. How could the practice of Rant, Rave, Repent, and Revel enhance your family connection?
2. What are some ways you can intentionally encourage your family members throughout the week?
3. When do you feel most seen or known by the members of your family?

Chapter 7:

Foundational Aspects of God's Nature

Many heartbroken Christian parents over the years have lamented to me, "Why can't my child see LGBTQ+ topics through a godly perspective?" And my response to them is always the same: "Do they even know who God is?"

Considering that sex, sexuality, and gender are deeply ingrained in the human experience (and thus, the Christian journey), typically, Christian parents exercise great care in broaching these intricate subjects with their children. Many Christian parents have asked, "How can I teach my children about LGBTQ+ topics in a manner aligned with my Christian values?" This is a matter that warrants careful consideration, urging Christian parents to diligently equip ourselves to initiate our children into these sensitive and profoundly significant discussions.

However, the process of educating our children on these subjects requires at least a foundational comprehension of God. Attempting to educate our children about LGBTQ+ topics without a fundamental understanding of God's nature is like teaching a child calculus before addition. It is destined to fail.

Core Aspects of God's Nature

Gaining insight into the fundamental principles of God's nature compounds and evolves as we mature. These fundamentals provide a cornerstone of comprehension about God that enables our children to view intricate, multifaceted subjects (like LGBTQ+ topics) from a divine perspective. But this is an ongoing journey. We aspire to continually construct a framework of faith within our children's hearts, equipping them to eventually view any topic—related to LGBTQ+ discussions or not—with God as their focal point.

Unconditional Love. We want our children to first and foremost know that God definitively loves them and every other human perfectly and unconditionally. Marvel at the mystery and enormity of God's love with your children! Train them to see God in everything—every story in the Bible, every provision you have in your life, every difficulty that draws you nearer to him—point it all back to God and his love.

Our kids need to know that God loves them even more than we do. Now, don't get me wrong, we are dishing out heaping helpings of parental TLC, to be sure! But it's imperfect love, and it doesn't even come close to comparing to God's perfect, all-encompassing, eternal love. They need to know that we are *stewards* of God's love for them, yet imperfect representations of it.

Righteousness/Obedience. Only when our kids have some sort of foundational understanding of God's love does righteousness and obedience even begin to make sense. We don't just want our kids to know *what* we need them to obey as God's people, we want them to understand *why* we obey—because we love him.[25] We obey God even when we don't understand why he asks certain things of us because we trust that, as our Creator, he knows what's best for us.

Free Will. We also want our children to understand the free will that God gives each person to live any way they'd like to, even if it's not the way he has asked them to live. That's how much God loves us! He gives us the power to not love him back, to not obey him if we so choose.

Consequences. In tandem with free will, our kids need to know that none of us are free from the consequences of exercising our will however we'd like to.

Grace. Though we are all bound to the consequences of the choices of our free will, there is always the promise of grace, forgiveness, and redemption through repentance in Jesus.

These foundational aspects of God show up in our kids' everyday lives. When I tell my five-year-old not to touch the hot stove, he can't possibly understand why. He certainly doesn't like it. And he has the free will to disobey me. He is not free of the consequences of burning his hand if he does disobey, but he has the autonomy not to listen to me when I say, "Don't touch that!" I won't love him any less if he disobeys—but it would hurt him. And it would hurt me to watch him be hurt.

In the same way, God is not in the business of stealing our joy or making harsh, arbitrary rules for no reason regarding LGBTQ+ topics. He is saying, as our heavenly Parent, that he knows better than we do in the areas of sex, sexuality, and gender (and all other areas). And he is asking us, his children, to trust him, our Creator; to trust that he loves us and that his way is best for us, even if we don't like it, even if we don't agree, and even if we don't understand.

You and I, our children, and all other humans on this planet have the option to obey God's directives—or not. Though none of us are free from the consequences of those choices, it certainly does not change God's love for people, even when they choose to disobey—and it shouldn't change our love and respect for others either.

Applying the Fundamental Traits of God

Our children need help in developing a balanced understanding of these pillars of God's nature—love and righteousness, in tandem—or the *messy middle.* Instilling an overdeveloped sense of righteousness in our child's heart may tend toward judgement and a lack of grace. But instilling an overdeveloped sense of love and grace in our child's heart may neutralize their understanding of the need for righteousness and obedience to God's word.

Divorce was a taboo subject during my childhood. I came home from school one day and told my parents in hushed tones that my friend Sarah's parents were getting a [*timidly checks surroundings and whisper-spells*] d-i-v-o-r-c-e.

That night, during our family devotional, my mom explained what divorce was to clear up any misconceptions I may have had. My dad then explained that, though divorce is not something that God wants for his people (*righteousness*), not everyone lives by the same standard that we do (*free will*), and that's okay (*grace*). Though there may be some natural *consequences* from getting a divorce, we are called to love every person and treat them with kindness, dignity, and respect, no matter how they exercise their free will (*unconditional love*).

Finally, my parents helped to breed empathy and compassion in my heart for my friend and her family. My dad, a child of divorce himself, shared some of his experiences and insecurities around growing up in a family of divorce that helped me to construct a plan for how to communicate to my friend at school about this.

I am not suggesting that divorce is a perfect parallel to LGBTQ+ topics, as God does make some exceptions for divorce in the Bible, yet there is never an exception made for same-sex relationships or crossing gender boundaries.[26] However, I use this example to highlight the artful way in which my parents incorporated the core aspects of God's nature to help me have a balanced perspective on a culturally volatile topic of my childhood.

A God-Centered Approach to LGBTQ+ Topics

Taboo subjects can vary in different times and cultures, but the formula that my parents implemented to teach me about a sensitive issue can be used for us to teach our kids about LGBTQ+ topics.

Explain Through an Earthly Lens. When our kids come home and ask about certain words or concepts they are hearing outside our homes, we want to make sure that their unformed brains are not left to their own devices to try to make sense of these big, complicated, important topics. Explain plainly to them what "gay," "transgender," "LGBTQ+" or other terms they may encounter in our world mean. Use a matter-of-fact tone, free of judgement, condemnation, or celebration. Speak plainly, with words and concepts that are age-appropriate for them.

> **Example:** Ravi told you that he has two moms. That must have been confusing for you since you have one mom and one dad. But the truth is that, in our world today, there are people that have two moms or two dads. Sometimes you might hear people refer to this as a gay couple, a queer couple, or an LGBTQ+ couple or family.

Explain Through a Godly Lens. Once they understand what the term or the concept means in our world today, then we can help them see it through God's eyes. We want to do our best to interweave all the foundational characteristics of God's nature discussed above, helping to foster a balanced perspective in our children's hearts.

> **Example:** God says that two men or two women being married to each other is not what he wants for his people and, because we live for God, we don't live that way. However, not everyone lives the way we do, and that's okay. God allows people to choose how they live and what they do with their life. Just because some people don't live for God, do you think God loves them any less? No! Would he want them to be treated any differently? No!

Cultivate Empathy and Compassion. We can help our children to develop empathy and compassion for the people in their lives who are dealing with LGBTQ+ identities. By doing this, we are exemplifying for our kids something really important about God's nature—that love is not dependent on agreement. We don't have to agree with how someone lives to strive to see them through God's eyes, with love and compassion.

> **Example:** A lot of people tend to mistreat and judge families that have two moms or two dads. We know that's not how God would have us treat them. But can you imagine what Ravi and his moms might have endured due to that bias? Some people may have tried to invalidate the love that Ravi's moms have for each other or for him. That would be really hurtful and wrong. That might lead anyone to feel unsafe about being open about something as fundamental as their own family.

Make a Plan. Once our kids are empathically attuned to the challenges that the LGBTQ+ community might face, they will be more adept at formulating strategies for respectful interactions with that community.

> **Example:** You can be a safe place for Ravi. Just talking to him openly and lovingly about his family could be a great way to show him that you love and respect him and his family. What are some other ways you can show Ravi and his moms respect and love, even though they live differently than we do? What do you think Jesus would do if he heard someone call Ravi or his moms something mean? What if Ravi were eating lunch all by himself in the lunchroom, what would Jesus have you do?

Knowing God

Let us never forget that one of our core responsibilities as God's stewards in our children's life is to help them really *know* our Lord. Not the mild-mannered, blond-haired, blue-eyed depiction of him that exists in some religious art. And not the cowboy renegade version of him that is often presented as steeped in contempt and condemnation for those that are not Christians. The *real* Lord—perfectly balanced between love and righteousness and between truth and grace.

This starts with *your* continual pursuit of knowing God deeply and intimately. Find a way to bring God into everything that happens in life. Intentionally draw your child's heart to God in everything they see and do. This is a great way to see God in everything yourself. I often hum the song, "Open the Eyes of My Heart" when I answer questions from my kids (e.g., "Why is the sky blue?" "Why is it raining?" "Why are men and women different?" etc.). When I am active in unveiling God's power and wonder to my children, I cannot help but see more of God myself. This has a spiraling effect in the best possible way. The more we see God, the more we want to see him. The more we want to see God, the more we will see him. This kind of hunger and thirst for God and desire for a deep, intimate knowing of him models exactly what we want to instill in our children's hearts—a deep desire to know, love, and be loved by God. It is from this intimate knowing of God that our children can then orbit a godly perspective in all facets of life, including when encountering LGBTQ+ topics.

 Reflect and Discuss

1. Which fundamental trait of God is hardest for you to grasp?
2. Apply the framework for navigating challenging conversations outlined in this chapter (worldly lens, godly lens, empathy, plan) to elucidate the process of addressing a different culturally sensitive subject with

your child (such as political disputes, abortion, cursing, etc.)

3. What are ways that you personally strive to know God deeply and intimately?

PART 3

Divine Design: Exploring God's Intent for Sex, Sexuality, and Gender

In this section we will explore the divine blueprint for intimacy, biological sex, and gender. This section is intended to help parents confront the distortions within their own heart so that they can teach their children God's design for sex, sexuality, and gender. Once we understand God's original design, we can then begin to make sense of modern deviations from it. This section will provide an overview of some salient terms in the LGBTQ+ discussion so that parents feel more confident in their ability to navigate LGBTQ+ conversations with their children. Utilize the foundations offered in the previous sections as you explore some of these sensitive topics with your children.

Chapter 8:

Sex and Intimacy

O ur Lord is complex, multilayered, and beyond our full comprehension, to be sure! Every part of his creation exists for multiple
purposes. Sex is no different.

It's true that one layer of the created intent for sex is procreation, as
Genesis 1:28 lays out. But there is another foundational and paramount
intent behind sex: to experientially understand but a glimpse of the kind
of intimacy and oneness that God desires to have with us. In Genesis 2:24,
God sets the expectation for marriage: "they become one flesh," thus creating a metaphor for the kind of oneness and intimacy that he desires to
have with *his* bride, the church.

Sex as an Element of Intimacy

The Bible is full of sexual language and euphemisms when referring to
God and his people. Just as the hearts and bodies of a husband and wife
become intertwined during sex, so God gives us his indwelling Spirit,

intertwining us with him. The New Testament elaborates on this metaphor in 1 Peter 1:23 and 1 John 3:9 by reminding us that God's seed is in us.

The Bible also uses sexual innuendo in Psalm 139, John 10:14, the whole book of Song of Songs, and many other places. For example, the biblical term *yada'* (Hebrew) or *ginosko* (Greek), conveys how God *knows* his people.[27] This isn't a surface-level knowing; this is a deep, intimate knowing that insinuates a *wink, wink*. These terms are used in places like Genesis 4:1 "Adam *knew* [wink, wink] Eve his wife, and she conceived and bore Cain" (NKJV, emphasis added). *Yada'*, translated here as "knew," is often translated as "lay with," as sexual union is the most intimate form of *knowing* that two humans can experience together.

God desires a level of intimacy with us that so far surpasses anything we experience as humans that our puny brains can't fathom it. Even the Apostle Paul calls the unfathomable love and devotion of God for us a "profound mystery" (Ephesians 5:32). The closest we can get to understanding the type of love and connection God wants to have with us is sex. So God uses language and connections that we can relate to in order to give us a glimpse into the kind of intimacy he wants with us.

Through this metaphor, God communicates the kind of pleasure, freedom, curiosity, vulnerability, trust, creativity, playfulness, risk-taking, desire, responsiveness, and surrender that he wants in a relationship with us. *This* is the Hebrews 4:13 kind of love that I was equally terrified of and intrigued by as a young teenager. *This* is true intimacy. Marriage and sex were created to point toward *this* kind of intimacy—not to replace or surpass it as the deepest form of intimacy. Sex in marriage provides but an echo of the kind of all-encompassing intimacy that God offers to each one of us.

The Desecration of Sex

My hand shot up when my graduate school Human Sex and Sexuality professor asked, "Who thinks God belongs in the bedroom with you and your spouse?" I looked around at my classmates, all brothers and sisters in the faith, and *not one other hand was raised.* When I got home from class that day, I wept. Not because I was embarrassed that my hand was the only one that was raised, but because I was grief-stricken at how Satan has robbed us of God's plan for sex and intimacy.

Stand in the remnants of Eden with me as we survey our current reality:

Intimacy lies broken, tattered, and stripped bare of all that God intended it to be. Instead of an experiential metaphor for the kind of oneness we were created for, the kind of oneness that appeals to the depths of our hearts, Satan has reduced intimacy to two lies:

1. Intimacy is just about sex.
2. Sex is just about physical attraction.

These two lies have dominated our world, controlled how we wield our sexuality, and denigrated connection.

What a frayed, thin concept for what God intended to be a rich and abundant form of intimacy.

Since the fall of humanity, the pure and essential elements of sexuality (pleasure, freedom, curiosity, vulnerability, trust, creativity, playfulness, risk-taking, desire, responsiveness, and surrender)[28] have been replaced by fear, doubt, and shame.

The trajectory of shame was laid out in Genesis 3—doubt gave way to desire for Eve, which gave way to sin for Adam and Eve, which ushered in shame for all of humankind, and thus disconnection between God and his creation. This is the legacy in which we now exist. Instead of being encompassed by a naked and unashamed existence with God and others, we are shrouded in doubt, fear, and shame—starved for *real* connection and intimacy, but terrified of the vulnerability required to pursue it.

Historically, we as God's ambassadors on this earth have stood up to Satan's widespread defilement of sex with a paltry, "Just don't do it before you're married, and you'll be fine." That is the *only* caveat we have put on this complete debasement of God's created intent!

Typically, Christian church traditions have even leaned on toxic purity culture that aims to discourage sexually impure actions through the use of shame, fear, and guilt as control mechanisms. If we perpetuate these distortions in sex education with our children, we equally mar sex and sexuality for them. Instead, we must reclaim God's original intent for sex and intimacy. Though we cannot go back and fix Satan's desecration of sex, as it is not *our* job to restore Eden on this earth, we must seek to embrace God's design as best we can in a fallen world, continually aligning the stewardship of our sexuality and our children's sexuality with the Creator's intent.

Divine Guidelines for Sex

My husband and I recently bought a new washing machine. After spending that much money (which is representative of a much more precious commodity, our time), you better believe we thoroughly read through the instruction manual to ensure that we would attend to our new purchase according to its creator's instructions. If it is expected and appropriate for us to take such great care of our things, which will not last, how much more attentive should we be to the Creator's instructions on concepts far more precious? If we want to steward our lives and our children's lives toward God, we ought to have a healthy understanding of his intention for connection, intimacy, and therefore, sex.

Scripture is abundantly clear that God's design is for sexual intimacy to be exclusively reserved between one man and one woman in a lifelong, monogamous marriage covenant. Several scriptures corroborate this truth: Genesis 19; Leviticus 18:22; Leviticus 20; Romans 1:24–27; 1 Corinthians 6:9–10; and 1 Timothy 1:9–10. Though theologians have spent an enormous amount of time debating the translation, meaning, and hermeneutics of these scriptures, we find the only proof we need in the very *beginning* of human existence. We will discuss more in Chapter 9 how sexuality is the *genesis* (see what I did there?) of relationship, connection, and intimacy. It is only fitting that God addresses the proper stewardship of our sexuality right from the start.

In Genesis 2:18–22, God is forming the pinnacle of his creation— Eve. Together with Adam, Eve will make up the full image of God. Just as we are witnessing a crucial moment in the history of creation, we see this important injunction on how to navigate this type of relational intimacy:

> *"This is now bone of my bones*
> *and flesh of my flesh;*
> *she shall be called 'woman,'*
> *for she was taken out of man."*
> **That is why** *a man leaves his father and mother and is*
> *united to his wife, and they become one flesh.*
> (Genesis 2:23–24, emphasis added)

God directly references the sex difference of Adam and Eve as the premise for entering this exclusive, one-flesh union. This statute is reiterated in Matthew 19:4–5, where Jesus references Genesis 2 and lays the foundation for sexuality in the new covenant. He says, "Haven't you read…that at the beginning the Creator 'made them male and female,' and said, '*For this reason* a man will leave his father and mother and be united to his wife, and the two will become one flesh'?" (emphasis added).

For what reason? Because God made them *male* and *female*.[29] There it is. Plain and simple. In both the Old Testament and the New Testament, in both covenants, God lays out the expectation for how to steward our sexuality, and it is directly related to sex difference. We are to be in a one-flesh union *only* with an opposite-sex spouse in marriage. God set this precedent in the very beginning and reminded us thousands of years later through Jesus that it still stands and is therefore prescriptive for all generations of God's people.

Preparing Kids for Sex Education

We must reclaim God's definition of intimacy. We need to help our kids see that living for God is not about saying "no" to sex, homosexuality, or sexual impurity of any kind. It's about saying "yes" to God's way. If he is the Creator of our bodies, our sexuality, and of sex itself, then he knows how it's best experienced.

We don't need to resort to scare tactics with our kids to terrify them into obedience to God's way. Instead, let's properly uphold God's beautiful and true intent for sex and sexuality so that our kids can *aspire* toward obedience in this, not *resign* themselves to it. Let's share with them (age appropriately) how much more fulfilling and satisfying sex is when it's done God's way.

One of the best ways to help children understand the biblical sexual[30] and gender ethic is to educate about the body appropriately. We can even start this with our kids from birth. I encourage parents to do three things when teaching their kids about the body.

1. **Speak About the Body Without Shame.** That means no euphemisms or nicknames for any body part. God created our body—all of our body—and there is absolutely no shame in any part of it. Even if the world has shamed or overly sexualized certain parts of the body, we as God's people do not hold to that distortion. We hold to biblical truth—and the truth is that there is no shame in God's intent for our bodies. Teach your children about the body in a matter-of-fact, shame-free tone that seeks to educate them about the mystery of their own bodies.

   > **Example:** You're noticing that your penis is larger in the morning. That's normal. It's called an erection. That means your brain has signaled for more blood to go to your penis, and that makes it erect. There's nothing shameful about it.

2. **Wonder in Awe at the Body Together.** Invite your child(ren) to wonder with you at the marvel of God and how he created our bodies. I recently told my five-year-old, "God made our bodies so that when we eat, our body takes what it needs and then gets rid of the rest. Isn't that amazing?" If I can make pooping a wonder-filled concept with my kid, you can do it with anything! Embrace a wonder-filled awe yourself as you encourage the wonder in your children through a shame-free education about the body.

> **Example:** When mommies are pregnant with babies, God made it so that the mommy's body feeds the baby's body. And when a baby feeds from their mommy's body, it bonds them together. Isn't that so cool how God did that?! God is so imaginative and creative in how he made us and our bodies!

3. **Teach That Certain Parts Need Extra Protection.** Our kids need to know that our bodies are full of wonder and that there is no shame in them. But we also need to teach them that certain parts of our bodies are more vulnerable and therefore need extra protection. We see this in 1 Corinthians 12:23–24 when Paul talks about the different parts of the body of Christ: "The parts that we think are less important we treat with special honor. The private parts aren't shown. But they are treated with special care. The parts that can be shown don't need special care. But God has put together all the parts of the body. And he has given more honor to the parts that didn't have any" (NIRV).

Our kids need to know that there are private parts of our bodies that deserve extra honor and protection. There is no shame in them, but because they are more honorable, they need extra special care. This education starts from birth and compounds as our children get older and are better able to understand more intricate topics regarding the body, sex, sexuality, and gender.

For example, a toddler cannot grasp the complexities of gender identity, but they can absolutely comprehend that God created women with vaginas and men with penises. This is where proper education on sex, sexuality, gender, and gender identity begins. Highlight the God-given differences between men and women with your children, never adding to these differences with rigid gender stereotypes that God did not implement or intend.

As your child matures, you can continually expound upon this education about the body to teach them about sex, then sexuality, then gender and gender identity (we will cover these in depth in the following chapters). See Appendix 2 for guidelines on when to teach your child about sex.

Reflect and Discuss

1. What surprises you most about God's intent for sex?
2. What are some things that may have affected your perspective of romantic and sexual attraction growing up?
3. How has toxic purity culture (unrealistic and often unbiblical standards of purity) affected you or your children?

Chapter 9:

Sexuality

A frustrated client once asked, "What even is sexuality?" This expansive term can sometimes feel nebulous and difficult to comprehend. Sexuality provides the bedrock for intimacy of all kinds. As Dr. Doug Rosenau puts it, "God wanted to reveal himself and the value he places on intimate loving relationships, so he created sexuality."[31] Rosenau attributes characteristics like joy, excitement, trust, commitment, unselfish nurturing, self-esteem, and mutually fulfilling companionship to sexuality.[32]

You see, sexuality is a foundational mechanism that God gave us to connect with him, to connect with others, to connect with ourselves, and to connect with the rest of his creation. No wonder Satan has attacked sexuality so aggressively! If sexuality is a cornerstone in deep connection, Satan has a lot to gain from the total and complete debasement of it. Navigating conversations with our kids about sex, sexuality, gender, and LGBTQ+ topics requires more than just understanding God's plan; it also requires a degree of awareness as to the contemporary misconceptions and distortions that surround sexuality.

Modern Terms

The terms within the LGBTQ+ conversation are continually prolif-crating and morphing. Encountering some of these terms can be daunting. We must strive for a balance here. These are terms that have been created to describe, as specifically as possible, an earthly designation that is not central to our identity in Christ. Therefore, as exiles on this earth, we do not need to become all-consumed with this language and commit to memory every single new term within this conversation. However, it behooves us as God's ambassadors to have a foundational understanding of some of the more prominent terms so that we can better communicate with the people of this world. I wonder if this is part of what Paul meant when he called us to be all things to all people.[33] If we do not learn the language of the world, how can we communicate with the people of this world about God? In that spirit, here are some foundational terms within the conversation about sexuality:

- ❖ **Gay:** a sexual or romantic attraction exclusively to people of one's own sex
- ❖ **Straight:** a sexual or romantic attraction exclusively to people of the opposite sex
- ❖ **Lesbian:** a reference to a woman who has exclusive romantic or sexual attractions to other women
- ❖ **Bisexual:** sexual or romantic attraction to both men and women
- ❖ **Asexual:** an umbrella term that indicates a lack of sexual attraction toward others (though romantic, intellectual, and occasional or slight sexual attraction can still be present)[iii]
- ❖ **Pansexual:** a sexual or romantic attraction to people regardless of their sex or gender

---

iii   Asexual has a different definition in the field of biology (an organism that can reproduce without the fusion of gametes). The definition of asexual offered in this book solely describes the meaning within the LGBTQ+ context.

❖ **Sapiosexual:** sexual or romantic attraction to another's intelligence

❖ **Demisexual:** sexual or romantic attraction that develops after establishing a close emotional bond with another

These terms give LGBTQ+ individuals a starting point to identify their personal experience with their sexual orientation and allow them to experience a sense of community and belonging among others who experience similar patterns of attraction. Sexual attraction is very confusing for many humans, especially given the amount of distortion that exists in our world around it. As Christians, we can have empathy for people who, swirling in confusion over their sexual attraction and desperately seeking an identity, have clung to these modern terms to try to make sense of and convey their patterns of attraction to others. However, we cannot stop at these terms. We must seek to understand the story—the heart—of the individuals using them. Understanding the heart means getting genuinely and non-judgmentally curious about another's experience and doing our best to see it through the eyes of God. When our kids see us interacting with LGBTQ+ language in a loving, compassionate way, like Jesus, they are better equipped to find the messy middle space as they contextualize LGBTQ+ topics from a godly perspective.

When our children witness us engaging with LGBTQ+ terminology in a loving and respectful manner, while still clinging to the truth, they become more adept at navigating the nuanced territory of LGBTQ+ discussions through a godly perspective. When our children observe us prioritizing the person and their character over the labels they apply to themselves, we are exemplifying that messy middle space, a space characterized by both love and righteousness. A place where Jesus resolutely stood.

Sexual Attraction vs. Sexual Action

Though romantic and sexual connection for God's people is to be reserved between one man and one woman in marriage, attraction to the same sex is never described as sinful in the Bible. I cannot control who

I am attracted to any more than you can. I never chose to be attracted to women. In fact, I've never met anyone who consciously chose to be attracted to a certain gender. Attraction just *is*. It's a neutral reality.

It's what we *do* with that attraction that can become sinful or righteous. The same is true for many different aspects of the human experience. For example, I am a very angry person by nature. Feeling anger in and of itself is certainly not sinful; it is a neutral reality. It is what I *do* with my anger that determines whether I will serve myself or God with it.

The Bible never says, "Do not be angry." Rather, it says, "In your anger do not sin."[34] The same could be said for same-sex sexual attraction. It's not, *Do not be attracted to the same sex*, but rather, *In your same-sex sexual attraction, do not sin.* This charge is not exclusive to the same-sex attracted. No matter what gender we are attracted to, if we live our lives for God, we are all held to the same sexual ethic—to not sin in the wake of our sexual temptations and desires, no matter whom they are geared toward.

It is certainly not sinful or even shameful for my husband to be attracted to another woman, but it would be sinful for him to lust after her, sleep with her, or engage in an emotionally enmeshed relationship with her. In the same way, it is not sinful or shameful for me to be attracted to another woman, but it would be sinful for me to lust after her, sleep with her, or engage in an emotionally enmeshed relationship with her. No matter which gender I am attracted to, if I choose to live my life for God, I am called to strive toward avoiding sin in my attraction toward another.

As my friend Guy Hammond likes to say, our goal is not to be heterosexually attracted, our goal is to be holy.[35] Our kids must understand that our biggest hope for them is not rooted in their sexuality. Our biggest hope for them is rooted in their intimacy with God. We want to help them strive toward holiness, regardless of their sexual orientation.

Developing a High View of Celibacy

To properly understand sex, sexuality, and intimacy, we must first reclaim God's definition, intent, and positive understanding of celibacy. If sex is the movie trailer for the feature film of deep intimacy with God,[36] celibacy is the sneak preview to it. As we discussed in Chapter 8, sex and marriage serve as symbols for the kind of intimacy we are created to experience with God. They represent only an echo of the ultimate outcome. But if earthly marriage and sex offer an echo, celibacy offers a whisper.

Sexuality serves as a means by which every human establishes deep connection with others,[37] particularly God. That means that celibate individuals are still sexual beings, yet they are liberated from the distortions of earthly sexual intimacy and are freed up to experience a profound intimacy with God in a way that married individuals cannot this side of heaven.

Many people assume that if a Christian experiences same-sex attractions and wishes to abide by the biblical sexual ethic, they must be celibate. As a same-sex attracted, non-celibate, happily married Christian in a *mixed-orientation marriage* (an opposite-sex marriage where at least one partner is attracted to the same sex), I would say that this is absolutely not true, as (1) sexual fluidity does exist. Often people who are same-sex attracted can experience some level of attraction to a spouse of the opposite sex. Even if physical attraction is not possible, romantic, emotional, or spiritual attraction may exist, thus aiding in the couples' overall connection and intimacy. And (2) there is nothing in the Bible that indicates that attraction is a prerequisite for marriage. If you have attraction within your marriage, that's great! But it's a very Western premise that attraction has to precede connection and romantic love. I have counseled many couples, and I don't know a single one that experiences attraction within their marriage every minute of every day. In fact, in my observation, relationships in which attraction is the main foundation of the couple's connection tend to suffer more quickly—after the initial infatuation and physical attraction have subsided.

Attraction waxes and wanes throughout the course of a marriage. Healthy marriages ought to have multiple points of connection that constitute overall intimacy: friendship, shared values, shared faith, appreciation for one another, shared experiences, trust, etc. If a marriage is too reliant on sexual attraction to create intimacy, the couple may neglect other essential points of connection, resulting in an insecure and uneven foundation. Being part of a mixed-orientation marriage can be an incredible gift that allows the couple to build the foundation of their connection on much stronger, more secure, and more godly constructs, instead of becoming too reliant on physical or sexual attraction.

But most importantly, as Christian parents, we must prioritize comprehending, appreciating, and revering the notion of celibacy as we seek to impart a profound understanding of genuine intimacy with God in our children's hearts. Celibacy is meant to be a gift from God—a gift somewhat like Sabbath. My family and I just started practicing Sabbath one day per week. I've always felt a bit apprehensive about the idea of observing the Sabbath because I've seen it as a restrictive way of life meant to stymie my natural hurried state of efficiency. But something fundamentally changed for me when I learned (through John Mark Comer's book *The Ruthless Elimination of Hurry*) that Sabbath is not a confining, unpleasant command meant to limit my week's productivity. It is a *gift* from God that aids in my connection with him, with creation, and with my heavenly home.

In the same way, we have misunderstood celibacy and painted it in a dull, constricting, and unappealing light. I've often heard people say, "I just don't have the gift of celibacy," as if it's akin to a fruit of the Spirit and some people have what it takes to be celibate, but others don't. Self-control is a fruit of the Spirit, and according to Paul, if a person lacks self-control in their sexual conduct, they ought to consider marriage in order to maintain purity and righteousness.[38] Celibacy, however, does not require some extraordinary superpower; celibacy, like Sabbath, *is the gift*.

This is what Paul tells us in 1 Corinthians 7 when he is explaining the benefits of celibacy: an undivided devotion to God, fewer worldly things to consume our minds and hearts, less earthly anxiety, etc. In the history of modern Christianity, we have done a poor job at upholding celibacy with the proper reverence and appreciation for the gift that it is.

Celibacy does not have to be an involuntary, shameful, resigned state of life. It was meant to be an exuberant, joyful, whole, and complete way of living that allows an individual to experience the many gifts that come from an undivided devotion to our Lord. Guiding our children toward a comprehensive understanding of sex, sexuality, and intimacy necessitates holding celibacy in high regard, as it brings us closer to the full picture of intimacy with God than sex and marriage alone.

Reflect and Discuss

1. When do you remember first being aware of your romantic or sexual attractions toward another person? What was it like to become aware of these desires?
2. How would you describe sexuality in your own words?
3. How was celibacy taught to you? What distortions exist around celibacy for you?

Chapter 10:

Gender

One of the very first things we see in Scripture is God claiming us as his image bearers.[39] Isn't that amazing?! He is the Creator of all things: the sun, the moon, the stars, the ocean, love, relationship, beauty, nature, everything that evokes strong emotion and awe from us—God created them.

All these awe-inspiring things are described as "good," to be sure! But the only affirmation of "very good" goes to the pinnacle of God's creation—his image bearers.

Just as a surge of pride and affection swells through your heart when you see your child imitate you in something, so God's heart swells when we represent but a single aspect of his full image. Let that sink in! When you desire justice, show mercy, love deeply, persevere, forgive, practice hospitality or righteousness—anytime you reflect God's character, the unseen audience of the heavenly host fondly lets out a figurative, "Aww, she looks just like her dad when she does that!"

Applying Scripture

I've had several conversations with people who have asked, "What scripture specifically references the topic of gender/transgender in the Bible?" Well, answering that question is not that easy. Before you slam this book shut in the name of *sola Scriptura*, just hear me out. If I were to ask you what scripture specifically addresses anorexia, you wouldn't be able to give me a book, chapter, and verse, although you could immediately confirm that anorexia is not congruent with the way that God wants his people to live.

You might point me to scriptures like 1 Corinthians 6:12–20 that talks about honoring God with our bodies; 1 Corinthians 6:19 that reminds us that our bodies are temples of the Holy Spirit; 1 Chronicles 22, 28, and Exodus 25–27 that discuss the diligent care expected when creating and maintaining other structures that house the presence of God on earth; Song of Songs 4:7 that mirrors the tender, unconditional love that God has for us just the way we are; and 1 Peter 3:3–4 that reminds us that beauty comes from within, not from the outward standards of the world.

Similarly, when attempting to understand God's will for us as it relates to gender and gender identity, there is not just one scripture that specifically addresses this question. A conglomeration of scriptures can inform this very culturally nuanced topic. My favorite description of the biblical tenets surrounding transgender identities is from Preston Sprinkle's research. This and the following chapter are heavily influenced by his work.

Divine Guidelines for Gender

Just as with our sexuality, the guidelines that God gives us relating to our gender are expressly stated in the very beginning: *"So God created mankind in his own image, in the image of God he created them, male and female he created them"* (Genesis 1:27, emphasis added).

Do you see how this sentence crescendos? It was a common Hebrew literary tool to accentuate a point and build up to the ultimate aim. Each repetition amplifies the one before and leads up to the unveiling of the full weight of the point in the end. In this sentence, the author is making a clear correlation between us being made in the image of God and our gender; they are intimately, intentionally, and *essentially* related.[40] God is making it clear to his creation that our biological sex is a part of the amazing gift we've been given to serve as image bearers of the great I AM.

> **So God created mankind in his own image, in the image of God he created them; male and female he created them.**
> (Genesis 1:27, emphasis added)

The Binary

Although Genesis 1 provides a foundational picture of what God created, not an all-inclusive encyclopedia on God's creation, there is a very clearly stated expectation of a sex binary: male *and* female. This expectation is reiterated throughout Scripture when humans are continually referred to in binary categories, like "husbands and wives" or "brothers and sisters." In fact, we never see a reference to a gender outside this binary in the Bible.[41]

Throughout the Bible, any deviation from established gender boundaries is consistently portrayed in a negative light. For example, 1 Corinthians 6:9 uses the term *malakoi,* which means "soft" or "effeminate," to refer to the passive partner when forbidding male same-sex sexual encounters.[42] Many scholars believe this term encompasses men who behave like women, thus crossing gender boundaries and breaking the gender binary that God calls us to live in.[43]

Binary Harmony

We can't fully know *why* the gender binary is essentially linked to our reflection of God, because it is not expressly stated in Scripture. However, God does choose to show us the very intentional and amazing harmony that he designed between men and women. Twice in Genesis, Eve is referred to as a "suitable helper" using the Hebrew word *kenegdo.*[44] This word is made up of two Hebrew words, *ke,* meaning "alike," and *neged,* meaning "opposite."[45] The author of Genesis is clearly illustrating the *ke* (sameness) of Adam and Eve, as they are both humans, and the *neged* (difference) of Adam and Eve, as they are male and female—two parts of one whole that come together to make up the full image of God.[46]

We see this concept in another important way God reveals himself to us—the Holy Trinity. God is all three: (1) Father, (2) Son, and (3) Spirit; they are the *same* (*ke*), but they are also *different* (*neged*).[47] They are each whole and complete within themselves, but they come together to create a more absolute whole—God. Similarly, God created man and woman, whole within themselves, but together making up a more perfect whole that more fully mirrors God's perfect image.

As God introduces this apex of creation—the human race—in the Bible, he makes it clear from the very start that his full image cannot be reflected by humans without the gender binary that he created. It's not men alone or women alone but the two halves of the human race, man and woman *together*, that make up the full image of God.[48]

This is even biologically evident in the way that God created us. As Christopher West's *Our Bodies Tell God's Story* puts it, "Every cell in a man's body has forty-six chromosomes…except for one. Every cell in a woman's body has forty-six chromosomes…except for one. The sperm cell and the ovum each have only twenty-three. Man and woman are meant to complete each other."[49]

If God is the perfect embodiment of male and female *together*, and if God created marriage to reflect his relationship with his bride, the church, then two men or two women cannot perfectly reflect the image of God. The binary is therefore essential to how we fulfill our function of image bearers and our ultimate glory as the bride of Christ.

The Body

Although this idea is anticultural in today's way of thinking, the Bible clearly portrays that the body and the soul are interwoven. Our bodies are part of who we are, not independent of our sense of self. The body and soul are integral elements of existence that are two parts of one whole—the self. Paul exemplifies this very idea in Romans 12 and 1 Corinthians 6 when he uses the terms "your bodies" and "yourselves" interchangeably as he calls people to righteousness. Our bodies are not independent of our sense of self; they *are* our self.[50]

Not only is this truth expressed by Paul in the New Testament, but it is also apparent from the very beginning. Genesis 2:21–22 often translates the Hebrew word *tsela* as "rib" when describing how Eve was created from Adam. However, in the forty(ish) other times the word *tsela* is used in the Bible, it usually refers to the side of a sacred building or structure, like the temple.[51] So Adam and Eve's bodies were compared to a sacred structure that houses the presence of God on earth, thus perfectly illustrating the way in which body and soul are interwoven.

We know that altering any other structure that houses the presence of God (the tabernacle, ark of the covenant, or temple) in a way not ordained by God was cause for extreme punishment.[52] Considering God's consistent nature, we can make the correlation that doing the same to our bodies would be equally forbidden and harmful to us and to God, especially since God took such care in creating our bodies. (Just read Psalm 139 for proof!)

In fact, God took such care in creating our bodies that they are meant to last even beyond this lifetime. Though 1 Corinthians 15:42–44 indicates that we will undergo some changes when our mortal bodies are resurrected into spiritual bodies in heaven (perishable to imperishable, dishonor to glory, weakness to power, natural to spiritual), there is nothing to indicate that we won't be gendered beings, even in our heavenly bodies. In fact, 1 John 3:2 states that we will be like Jesus when we are resurrected into our spiritual bodies. Even Jesus was still sexed within the gender binary when he was resurrected.[53]

It is evident that God fashioned us as complete, incarnate beings, not mere spirits inhabiting bodies. There is a purpose to our bodies; they are intentional, sacred, and part of our personhood.[54] In fact, God has put such care into creating and intertwining our body and our being together that he even asks us to tremble in awe and wonder over them.[55] Clearly, our (gendered) bodies are integral to our very being. And our bodies were very intentionally put in a binary—a binary that God calls his people to uphold.

Preparing Kids for Gender Education

Teaching our kids about gender starts with teaching them about the body. They must first understand the differences between the male and female body (see Chapter 8). As we teach our children about the body and about gender, we want them to see us awestruck at the amazing way that God intertwined the concept of gender with both (1) his image and (2) our relationship with him.

Our children need to understand that gender is biological and bestowed by God. But they can also understand that because we no longer live in Eden, pain, brokenness, and distortion have made their way into our existence, and therefore, some people don't feel comfortable in their gender. It is possible to have compassion for those who experience incongruence with their gender while still holding to the concrete truth that God has laid out in the Bible regarding our biological sex (If it is your child that is struggling with an incongruence in their gender, see Chapters 2, 11, and Appendix 2).

We never want to teach our children something as a retaliation against what the world believes. Introducing our children to the concept of gender from a biblical lens does not need to be an "us versus them" conversation. Instead, our goal is to provide them with a comprehensive understanding that respects both truth and grace.

 Reflect and Discuss

1. What are your reactions to the biblical theology surrounding gender? What do you agree with? What do you disagree with?
2. Where does your theological stance on gender come from?
3. Describe your reaction to our bodies and souls being interwoven.

Chapter 11:
Gender Identity

N ow that we have an understanding of the theology of gender, we are better able to understand distortions of it. Transgender identification is one of the most contentious issues facing our modern world. Even within the church, I've come across a wide range of perspectives on the issue. I've encountered people who, red-faced and shaking, exclaim things like, "It's maddening! It's a man in a dress, not a woman!" and I've encountered people, equally vehement, exclaiming, "How dare we tell this person how they ought to feel and what is right for them!" These seemingly opposing views each embody an important divine perspective.

We want our children to have reverence for God's statutes surrounding gender, but we also want them to look at contemporary deviations from the truth with empathy and compassion, just like Jesus did with the contentious issues of his time. This is why the messy middle is imperative for this discussion. We must strive to stand on the firm ground of truth, but with copious amounts of grace and compassion in order to navigate this contentious terrain effectively.

Modern Terms

In Chapter 9 we discussed a balanced perspective when approaching modern terms within the sexual attraction conversation—not becoming consumed by the contemporary designations but having a healthy understanding of them in order to honor those in our world that use them. The same goes for this discussion about gender identity. There are an overwhelming number of terms in this discussion, and the list of those terms continues to grow. We, as God's people, do not need to become experts in these terms, but understanding them could help us better communicate with and connect with those who are experiencing gender identity incongruence. In that spirit, below are some terms that might be helpful for you to know in this discussion:

❖ **Transgender:** an umbrella term used to describe someone who identifies as a separate gender from the gender they were assigned at birth. As the spectrum of experiences under this umbrella term are vast (ranging from sentiments such as, "I'm a man trapped in a woman's body" to "I'm a natal female, but I don't like stereotypical feminine toys, colors, and activities"), it's important to dig beyond this term to find out someone's unique experience with their gender identity. No two people are alike; therefore, no two trans people are alike.

❖ **Trans Man/AFAB (Assigned Female at Birth):** born a female and now identifies as male.

❖ **Trans Woman/AMAB (Assigned Male at Birth):** born a male and now identifies as female.

❖ **Cisgender:** refers to a person whose gender identity corresponds with their biological sex.

❖ **Natal Sex:** the biological and physical sex characteristics an individual is born with, typically categorized as male, female, or intersex.

❖ **Sex:** biological and associated with reproductive organs and secondary sex characteristics (i.e., chromosomes, hormones, etc.).

❖ **Gender:** used to be used synonymously with "sex," but now is used to denote a range of identities with two main contributing components, gender identity and gender expression.

❖ **Gender Identity:** someone's personal, internal sense of their gender.

❖ **Gender Expression:** someone's external expression of their internal gender identity.

❖ **Nonbinary:** a designation someone could use to convey that they do not adhere to a strict gender binary (male and female). They may see gender as existing on a spectrum. This is another umbrella term that could encompass many different experiences and subterms.

❖ **Sexual Orientation:** references which gender or gender expression a person is sexually attracted to.

❖ **Intersex:** describes an extremely rare condition where someone is born with a physical abnormality in either their genitals or their secondary sex characteristics (chromosomes, hormones, etc.). Many intersex individuals do not want to be counted as part of the LGBTQ+ community, as they are dealing with an identifiable physiological medical issue. Though the discussion of intersex individuals lies outside the scope of this book, it is a relevant and extremely important conversation. If you'd like to learn more about it, I highly recommend Preston Sprinkle's *Embodied*.

❖ **Gender Dysphoria:** a clinical mental health diagnosis indicating that someone has marked incongruence over their biological sex and their gender identity. This incongruence is associated with marked distress that affects typical, everyday functioning.

❖ **Rapid-Onset Gender Dysphoria (ROGD):** a social subcategory within gender dysphoria that is a growing phenomenon among adolescents (12–18 years old), in which gender dysphoria springs up quickly and intensely. This designation tends to be more common in natal females and tends to include more of a social influence (e.g., YouTube, Tumblr, TikTok, peer influence, social media, TV, movies, etc.).[56]

Mark Yarhouse, a biblical scholar in the field of sexuality and gender, likes to say, "If you've met one person who is transgender, you've only met one person."[57] Though understanding the above terms can be helpful to us as Christians, they should never replace deep, meaningful conversation with another person to better understand their unique experience with their gender identity. Each person's experience is distinct and deserves its own safe place to be told. Therefore, when we hear a term from one person's mouth, we cannot assume that it expresses the same experience when used by someone else. We cannot rely on terms alone to understand the depths of someone's personal experience. We must dig beyond the term to find out the story.

Confronting Socially Constructed Gender Stereotypes

Though we find overwhelming support in the Bible that our gender exists in a God-ordained binary (see Chapter 10), there is no evidence that *living out* our gender exists in dichotomous categories. The Bible gives us many examples of faithful, righteous men and women who broke barriers of cultural expectations for their gender roles.

God himself contradicts our *socially constructed* gender stereotypes. He is the tender, deeply emotional God who refers to himself in a nurturing, maternal role, even identifying with a pregnant and nursing mother.[58] Jesus defies our earthly gender stereotypes by showing the depths of his emotion on multiple occasions. He cried.[59] He sometimes felt afraid.[60] He also referred to himself in a maternal role, longing to gather his people to him like a mother hen gathers and protects her baby chicks.[61]

Peter was excitable and often driven by his emotions.[62] The good Samaritan was tender and kind to someone in need.[63] How about mighty, masculine David who defeated Goliath with one rock and killed a lion with his bare hands? He was also the guy who tended to the sheep in the field while his brothers were off fighting a war.[64] He was the dancing, music-playing,[65] poetry-writing king who exuded tremendous emotion and vulnerability, even sobbing when he was about to be separated from his best friend.[66]

Deborah was a warrior who led men in battle.[67] Jael was *super* violent[68]—Jackie Chan had nothing on her! Ruth provided for her mother-in-law the way a son would, sweating and toiling in the fields, and she exuded boldness and courage in her pursuit of romantic love.[69] The soldiers in God's army looked to Rahab as she courageously stood with and protected them. Abigail was cunning and calculating in the way she confronted David, valiantly saving her entire household in the process.[70] The Proverbs 31 woman was a modern woman! She worked, provided for her family, and bought property.[71]

God is deliberate in presenting a comprehensive view of gender expectations as he showcases examples of righteous men and women. The Bible lifts up some incredibly mighty and powerful men and some very nurturing and tender women. But God is careful to also show us the tender side of masculinity and the fierce side of femininity.

Dangerous Effects of Rigid Gender Stereotypes

Unfortunately, a lot of our modern ideas of what masculinity and femininity require are not based on the Bible but rather on earthly notions. I felt ashamed while growing up because I didn't like wearing dresses, playing with Barbie dolls, or dreaming about what color napkins would be at my wedding. I wish I hadn't spent so much time fretting over these things because now as an adult, I don't see anything in the Bible that indicates these qualities are requirements for women. Though the Bible does have specific directives for men and women, they are far less numerous and constricting than the earthly expectations we have allowed to infiltrate our hearts, our homes, and our churches.

When our children encounter rigid gender stereotypes, shame and isolation can creep into their hearts. They can begin to feel how I felt as a young child: "Something is wrong with me; I don't belong among those of my same gender." This insecurity, coupled with the modern-day rhetoric surrounding transgender identities, could convince any child that there is a mistake with their God-given gender. We cannot allow rigid gender stereotypes to rule our expectations or our homes. These are often fueling transgender identities in our children.

We as a human race tend to overcorrect by swinging the pendulum way too far to the other side, and thus we continue to miss God's mark. We see this happening in our society right now with this very issue. There is a cultural push to make everything gender-neutral in an attempt to overcorrect historically rigid gender roles. Masculinity and femininity have been stripped bare and villainized in certain parts of our modern culture. *This is not the answer.*

There are general observations we can make about *most* men and *most* women regarding their masculinity or femininity. For example, men tend to have the ability to build greater muscle mass than women; women tend to excel in relational domains, like the ability to express empathy. Ignoring these generalities can be just as harmful as making them rigid expectations.

But it's important to recognize that these general observations of *most* men and women do not hold true for *every* man and woman. We would never tell a husband who couldn't bench press as much as his wife to bulk up with protein powder and bicep curls, lest he continue his sinful life of frailty, just as we would never tell a wife that had less emotional expression than her husband to listen to Adele on repeat until she cried. Imposing these generalizations as rigid criteria for expressing masculinity and femininity is not just erroneous, it has the potential to evoke feelings of shame in our children and, even worse, can lead to a distorted understanding of God's expectations for them.

Cultivating Image-Bearing Traits

Our distorted perspective on masculinity and femininity affects our own lives and everyone's lives around us—most devastatingly, *our children's.* We *must* be mindful of these unbiblical expectations we often unknowingly place on our children's expressions of masculinity or femininity. Let's stop only cultivating stereotypical masculine traits in boys and stereotypical feminine traits in girls. We cannot stuff gender into a box that God did not create.

As Preston Sprinkle points out, our goal in life is to have our character be more like Jesus, not more stereotypically masculine or feminine.[72] So let's not limit our character-building to the attributes that stereotypically line up with our gender. That said, let's also not *deny* our natural abilities, even if they comply with cultural stereotypes. Instead, let's embrace all our godly characteristics by correlating our character with that of Jesus, not other men or women.

I wish I had heard more of this kind of sentiment growing up:

"Wow, Ellen! You are so passionate and indignant, just like when Jesus flipped over the tables in the temple!"

OR

"Whoa! You are so direct! What a gift! Just like when Jesus called the Pharisees whitewashed tombs. Maybe you could incorporate more of Jesus' love next time, but WOW! I see you being an image bearer to Christ in your zeal, in your indignation, and in your boldness!"

If I had heard affirmations like these when I was growing up, perhaps I would not have convinced myself that my passion and directness are "manly traits," good for a man to have but shameful for me to have.

Proper education regarding gender and gender identity not only seeks to dismantle gender roles that are too rigid but also correctly highlights the distinctions of each gender. Instruction about the differences in gender starts with proper education about the body (see Chapter 8). We should emphasize the inherent distinctions between men and women to our children, even acknowledging observable generalities, but never impose rigid gender stereotypes that were not ordained or intended by God.

If you need to teach your child about a cultural norm, try to do it without tying it to a gender role. For example, my parents used to tell me that I needed to "eat like a lady." This was confusing to me as a child because, as far as I could tell, digestion worked pretty much the same for both men and women. Tying it to a gender role was confusing. However, "Sweetie, it's impolite to chew with your mouth open" is a great way to teach your kids (male or female) about cultural norms without invoking a rigid gender stereotype that could be shame-inducing.

Use your times of intentional connection with your kids to highlight their image-bearing traits from God. Look at different men and women in the Bible and pinpoint the characteristics that mirror God. Show your kids that your hope is not for them to become a more (stereotypically) masculine man or a more (stereotypically) feminine woman. Your hope for them aims much higher—to become more like Jesus.

 ## Reflect and Discuss

1. What are some of your favorite biblical examples of breaking gender stereotypes?
2. How did rigid, socially constructed gender stereotypes affect you while growing up?
3. What characteristics did God give you that echo his nature? How about your children?

Chapter 12:

Love: The Essential Anchor in LGBTQ+ Education

A lot of professing Christians like to stop the discussion of homo-sexuality and transgender identities at, "It's sinful." They treat this theology on sexuality and gender like it trumps all other theology, ignoring the theology even more foundational to God's creation: *love*. The theologies on sexuality and gender do not negate our charge to love every part of God's creation and to treat every person with reverence, respect, kindness, and dignity. No matter their theological interpretation, no matter their sexual orientation, no matter their political affiliation—*no matter what*—we are to love.

Consider Jesus' example in this area. The socially contemptible people of his day—the sinners and tax collectors, the fringe outcasts of his society—they sought him out![73] Think about that. Jesus didn't go chasing after them. He didn't scream obscenities at them while picketing against their life choices. He simply welcomed all and loved all...and they gathered around him to learn the truth, even though it directly contradicted the way they were living. Let us never forget that our first charge is *to love*.

My First Gay Pride Experience

This kind of love is a far cry from the example of Christianity that I saw during my time as part of the LGBTQ+ community. I remember my first Gay Pride parade. I was an eighteen-year-old non-Christian, and I was nervous and excited to be attending my first Pride parade.

I didn't have the guts to go by myself, so I had a friend who had gone before accompanying me. I had recently come out and did not know what to expect in terms of acceptance within the LGBTQ+ community. I felt like a five-year-old preparing to go to kindergarten for the first time. "What will it be like?" "Will they like me?" "Will they think I'm weird?"

There was no wild or scandalous desire in my heart as I walked up to the crowds of people celebrating what they considered to be a big part of their identity—an identity that I shared at the time. I remember walking up to the mass of people thinking, "*These* are my people! *This* is where I belong! I *finally* found it!"

My confused, terrified, and disoriented heart was not trying to intentionally bring distress to God or his people—they weren't even on my mind. I was simply searching for a place to belong, for meaning, for something to help me make sense of what I was feeling. As I walked up to what I yearned to claim as "my people," my heart swelled with excitement and a growing sense of kinship with this group. As I got closer to the crowds, I felt like running to embrace this expanding sense of freedom and acceptance that I could feel emanating from them.

This sense of warmth, belonging, and acceptance felt reminiscent of the kind of camaraderie that I had always felt in church as a child. Growing up, I witnessed people who went out into the world every day and were persecuted because they chose to live outside cultural norms. These people, called "aliens," "foreigners," and "outsiders" in Scripture, had nerves of steel to be able to endure that kind of hardship day after day as they went out into a foreign land. Weary and misunderstood, they found great solace among a group of like-minded people where it felt safe to take off their armor and just *be*. The feelings of celebration, relief, and security were palpable as God's people came together on Sunday mornings. They were encouraged by one another as they reoriented to their core identities and learned from one another how to survive the challenges they faced as Christians.

I felt a similar anticipation and excitement as I walked up to my first Pride parade. I was eager to finally shed the sense of being an outsider and embrace the sense of belonging that I was convinced waited for me just beyond the entrance.

Suddenly, my attention was yanked from its reverie as I started to hear anger, disapproval, even animosity in the air. These things seemed out of place, so it took me a moment to notice the people all around the entrance holding up signs, screaming into megaphones, and literally standing on soapboxes.

Startled, I looked up at my friend the way a kindergartener would look up at their parent when they encounter an unexpected, harsh reality walking into their first day of school. My friend just shook her head, cast her eyes down, and hunched her shoulders in shame and defeat as she led me through the throngs of faces contorted with rage.

As I acclimated to this unexpected twist, my brain finally allowed me to hear what they were saying. To my shock, these people, these *Christians*—the people with whom I had identified so closely until that time in my life—were screaming words of *hate*, condemning the crowds, condemning my newfound community, condemning *me*.

I was heartbroken. I could not fathom why it was so important to those Christians to be there yelling at me—loathing me simply because I was choosing to pursue a path different from theirs.

"What did we do to them?" I asked my friend as we entered the parade. She had no answer.

The biggest knife to my heart was that the yelling Christians were holding *Bibles* as they screamed these words of hate and condemnation. I grew up in a Christian home with God and his word as the bedrock, so the Bible had always been a steady source of solace for me. I could not believe they were using the same words that I had grown up with, not to teach me and show me the way of God, but to oppose the word of God by condemning me in disgust and hate.

I could feel my heart harden in that moment, as it suddenly seemed impossible to separate a perfect God from these imperfect people. As they held his word to castigate me in my vulnerability, in this moment when I was desperately seeking a place to belong, the overall message from these ambassadors of Christ was not, "Christianity is where you *really* belong. Let us show you the way." Instead, their message was, "We don't know where you belong, but you definitely don't belong with God." I tear up even now, years later, remembering the utter devastation I felt in that moment.

Those professing Christians at my first Pride parade expressed their position so wrongfully that no one could see the truth in it. Although their theology was right—homosexuality (and transgender identification) is sinful—the condemnation they shouted did not stem from love. It stemmed from fear, anger, pride, and disgust. We can have the right belief, but if we express it without love, *we are still wrong*:

> If I speak in the tongues of men or of angels but do not have love, I am only a resounding gong or a clanging cymbal. If I have the gift of prophecy and can fathom all mysteries and all knowledge, and if I have a faith that can move mountains, but do not have love, I am nothing. If I give all I possess to the poor and give over my body to hardship that I may boast, but do not have love, I gain nothing. (1 Corinthians 13:1–3)

We must follow in Jesus' footsteps in *how* we profess our theology—we must share it in love, just as God commands.

Love Is a Matter of the Heart

The kind of love that God exemplifies for us and expects from us does not begin and end with controlling our tone or facial expressions to hide disapproval. Love is not simply behavioral modification; *love is a matter of the heart*. If God is love, then the first and most important thing we need to do in order to love others is to *draw nearer to him*.

Let us also remember that God does not call us to force the world to submit to his ways. God gives each of us the free will to choose how we would like to live. The free will that allows me to surrender my same-sex sexual desires to God for an identity in him is the same free will that God gives every human, even if they choose to indulge in their same-sex sexual attractions.

God's love does not change for people who do not live for him—and neither should ours. God calls us to judge only those within his kingdom (1 Corinthians 5:9–11). We are not called to judge those outside the church—that responsibility lies with God and God alone.

We can absolutely say that homosexuality is sinful. However, we can make no statements as to a person's character, heart, intention, or eternal destination, because that would put us in the position of God. That kind of judgement lies outside the scope of what we are capable of as mere humans. Praise be to the One who can judge perfectly and relieves us from such a great burden.

Finally, let us remember that LGBTQ+ people are *people*. They are fellow humans. Along with you and me, they make up the apex of God's creation. God wants each of us to treat his beloved creation with the kindness, dignity, and respect that a son or daughter of the Most High King deserves, no matter how they have chosen to exercise their God-given free will.

Words vs. Heart

Many Christian parents want to know exactly what to say to their kids when teaching them about LGBTQ+ topics. Though the words we use ought to be carefully and deliberately chosen, we can say the right words with the wrong heart and still miss the mark. The words are important, but there are much more important things to consider when teaching our kids about LGBTQ+ topics:

Show Up. Our kids are resilient and can handle our mistakes and our imperfect words. What they cannot handle is being left alone in trying to understand and process some of these sensitive topics. Even if you are bumbling through these conversations with your kids—celebrate victory! You showed up. You are walking alongside them in this, as the God-appointed spiritual steward in their life.

How vs. What. What you say is important, but *how* you say it is far more important. In ten years, your kids won't remember the words you used to teach them about sex, sexuality, gender, or LGBTQ+ topics. They *will* remember how they felt when you discussed these topics with them. Make sure your heart, and therefore your tone and words, are free of judgement, condemnation, shame, and fear when you have these sensitive discussions with your kids.

Out of the Overflow of the Heart. Every time a parent starts to worry about words, I always encourage them to go deeper—to the heart. God says that our words (and tone, inflection, timing, etc.) reflect what is in our hearts. When we place ourselves before God and take time to reflect on our own sin and shortcomings, reminiscing on the mercy, grace, and forgiveness he has bestowed on us, it is nearly impossible to sit in judgement of another. When we ruminate on God's providence and love in our lives, it's nearly impossible to see another without love and compassion. When we rededicate our lives and hearts to God, it's nearly impossible not to have the Holy Spirit guide our communication. These practices ought to be routine in our preparation for engaging in sensitive discussions with our kids. We must spend more time on preparing our frame of heart than our frame of mind. If our heart is set above, the rest will follow.

Confront Your Own Distortions. Chances are you personally have some distorted beliefs about the body, sex, sexuality, and gender. That's okay. We all do—we live in a broken world. Before you teach your kids about these tender topics, you may want to consider going to get help to correct some of the distortions that might exist in your own heart so that you don't unknowingly pass on some of those distortions to your kids.

Imperfectly Walking Alongside Your Children

Though it's important that we approach LGBTQ+ topics with our kids thoughtfully and with genuine emotional engagement, I want to relieve you of the pressure of doing this perfectly. You will *not* do it perfectly. You will mess it up. And that's okay. It's not our goal to do this perfectly, it's our goal to *do it*. Remember, we are stewards on this earth for our kids. That means we do the best we can with what we have—this allows us to have a clear conscience before God in our parenting. Not that we did it perfectly, but that we stood in the gap as God's proxy, and we gave it our all.

In fact, when we (inevitably) mess up, it's an opportunity to model humility, repentance, and perseverance for our kids. We *will* hurt our kids. Our kids *will* be affected by the pain and the brokenness in this world. The less we try to prevent that at all costs, the more we are freed up to teach them how to better navigate the inevitable pain and brokenness they will experience. *That* is our job as parents. Not to restore Eden for our kids; unfortunately we don't have that kind of power. There is room to mourn and grieve that. But then we need to get back up and do the only thing we can do—love our kids and teach them to navigate this distorted world with God at the center of their minds and hearts. *This* is what allows our kids to catch a glimpse into Eden while living in a world so far removed from it.

 Reflect and Discuss

1. Why do you think it is so scary for us to encounter beliefs that are different from our own?
2. Describe your reaction to the comparison drawn between the camaraderie and safety found in God's church and the LGBTQ+ community.

3. What distortions may be getting in the way of you discussing sex, sexuality, and gender freely and without shame with your kids?

4. Describe your reaction to the assertion that no parent will perfectly teach their kids about LGBTQ+ topics.

PART 4

Building Bridges: Parenting an LGBTQ+ Child

While the previous sections have addressed how to navigate LGBTQ+ *topics* in a Christian household, this section will focus on navigating a child's LGBTQ+ *identity*. In this section we will explore how parents can tether their hearts to God and gain the support they need to parent an LGBTQ+ child effectively. We will also discuss practical guidance on how to foster meaningful connection and effective communication with your LGBTQ+ child.

Chapter 13:

Grief and Support

"The LORD is close to the brokenhearted and saves those who are crushed in spirit."[74] I have yet to speak to a Christian parent of an LGBTQ+ child who is not gripped by immense grief, shock, guilt, fear, and shame when their child comes out.

There is an onslaught of emotion when you feel that your child blatantly rejects the biblical tenets you've spent a lifetime instilling in their hearts. It doesn't just feel like a rejection of God and his ways; it feels like a direct rejection of you, the parent. Parents I've spoken to usually have four categories of emotion that they are navigating when their child comes out to them:

Pain and Hurt

How could they reject me and God this way?

Why did they keep this from me for so long?

Fear

What else are they not telling me?

Are we not as close as I thought we were?

Are they pulling away from me?

What if they never have a relationship with God?

What if I don't see them in heaven?

Guilt

It's my fault.

If only I had _____.

Shame and Inadequacy

Are we bad parents?

Are we bad Christians?

What will our friends at church think?

It is impossible to navigate all these emotions and still live life as you did before your child came out to you. When a child comes out to their parents, the parents often enter a whirlwind of grief, shame, isolation, loneliness, and fear.

Complicated Grief

It is important for parents going through this to allow themselves to grieve. Stuffing our grief is never the answer; this only ensures that it will bubble up and come out at the worst possible time, often disguised as anger or despondence. We must actively engage in the grieving cycle.

Grief is difficult in any circumstance, but a child coming out qualifies as *complicated grief*. With more traditional grief, like when someone close to us dies, life as we know it stops. We don't have to go in to work for a time, people bring over meals, our friends don't get upset if we withdraw for a bit, our children give us space as we process and mourn, and our own expectations for ourselves are temporarily stripped down to the bare essentials as we move through the grief fog.

In grieving lost loved ones, we gain a sense of meaning and purpose as we notify friends and relatives, plan a celebration of life, and trudge through the wasteland of shock and denial. We receive a bit of comfort as we get cards, notes, and kind words about our loved one and the life that they lived. We are allowed a small sense of closure and finality when we attend funerals and memorials. This grief is difficult, but there is a socially constructed, ritualistic process our brains can latch on to as we ease into the much longer process of gradually accepting our new reality.

The type of grief that overwhelms us when our children come out to us is very different because those around us can't see what we're grieving. Our expectations of ourselves and others' expectations of us have not changed. We still go to work. We are still expected to care for ourselves, our kids, and others the same way we always have, even while we sluggishly move through the grief fog, often on autopilot. There are no words of comfort or assurances given, no ceremonies or cultural rituals to engage in to bring about any sense of closure or comfort.

This type of grief is also usually fast-tracked. Parents typically find out about their child's sexual or gender identity when the child has already had years to process it themselves. Often, children have friends that know and possibly even a whole different persona outside the home before they finally come out to their parents. This means that parents are often breathlessly running to catch up with their child's requests (which often feel like demands) regarding their sexual or gender identity. They must respond while emotionally, mentally, and spiritually limping from the grief they find themselves in, wounding themselves and their connection with their kids even further.

Tending to Grief

A client, Dakota, once described a powerful image that emerged during a period of mourning in her own life:

> I envisioned that I was in a colosseum, my heart shat-
> tered into a million glass fragments, scattered across the

sandy floor. There, alongside me in the dirt and sand knelt Jesus, slowly and gently collecting each shard of my shattered heart, cradling them, one by one. As he held the broken fragments of my glass heart, there were moments when they cut him, causing him to bleed. Together, we wept, as he acknowledged the pain each shattered piece held, saying, "I remember that. It was so painful. I was with you then, and I'm with you now."

Sometimes the answer is to retreat with God and allow him to tend to our woundedness. (Read 1 Kings 19 for a visual of how patiently and tenderly God yearns to care for your broken heart.) Just as you would if you were experiencing other kinds of grief, let life slow down a bit. Prioritize and prune any nonessentials in life during this time. Temporarily increase boundaries and decrease commitments as you move through this fog of grief. Allow people to serve you by bringing meals, sitting with you, or just being patient with you as you withdraw into God for a bit. Take time away to just *be* with God—sit with him and allow him to tend to your broken heart, to put the pieces back together as you fall apart before him.

Actively engaging in the grieving process takes intention. Healthy grieving does not mean lying in bed all day allowing yourself to be assailed by your emotions. It means intentionally going to God, intentionally expressing your primary emotions to him and other safe people, and intentionally communicating some boundaries to provide space and time for you to move through the initial thicket of emotions. Feelings are meant to be felt. Allow yourself to feel your big emotions.

Sometimes it may be necessary to schedule your grief. When something in your daily life reminds you of this underlying sorrow and you feel the grief begin to envelop you at a time when it's not safe to come out, tell it to come back later. Schedule a date with your grief: "Saturdays from 10 to 11 a.m. are my open-door grief hours. Please come back then and I will be sure that you are fully tended to and honored." At your regularly scheduled grieving window, sit before God and allow all the pent-up pain from the day or week to fully wash over you. "Blessed are those who mourn, for they will be comforted."[75] Lean into the grief and allow it to draw you nearer to God as he comforts you in a way only he can.

Support

As you're going through the *initial* grieving process (grief never ends, it changes and morphs over time), it will be important to activate your support system. You cannot do this alone; you will need a robust team around you to help lift your arms during this particular battle within your heart.[76]

Stay Connected to God

Your first line of defense in your support system is your relationship with God. This might be difficult. When something big like this happens in my life, I tend to feel hurt by God, forgotten, unprotected, and exposed. If you feel like this with God and are tempted to withdraw from him, tell him! God can handle it.

Fight for perspective as you draw nearer to God, even in your pain. Allow him to give you the strength that only he can. Allow him to see the most exposed and raw parts of your heart as you move through this. Ask him for perspective: "God, help me to see this situation through your eyes; help me to see my son or daughter as you do." And surrender everything—even your understanding—to him as you melt into the trust you have in his boundless love for you.

Connect with Your Spouse

If you are married, your second line of defense will be your spouse. LGBTQ+ issues in a Christian home have the potential to rip a marriage apart. I've seen it. *Don't let this be your family!* Intentionally connect with your spouse to keep Satan from getting a foothold here. Regularly create alone time with your spouse to talk about your grief, your emotions, your fears, and your hopes for your child. Validate your spouse's emotions and ask them to validate yours. Reflect back to each other what you hear each other saying.

Do *NOT* start blaming your spouse. Blaming someone else can alleviate our own feelings of inadequacy. Resist this common temptation. Instead, vulnerably expose to your spouse your own feelings. As you express your tender, primary emotions to them, ask your spouse what they are feeling and help draw out their primary emotional response. No one else on this earth knows what you're going through like your spouse does because they are going through the same thing.

Don't withdraw from them; lean into them. Inevitably, your spouse will view this differently than you do. That's good! *That's why you married them!* They are the yin to your yang, and you need their perspective just as they need your perspective to get through this. Listen and learn from your spouse and non-judgmentally reflect what you hear them saying.

Make time with your spouse to have fun and take a temporary break from your grief. When I was in college, one of my best friends, Maxine, lost her dad. It was devastating. I drove Maxine to her hometown as she geared up to take care of all the arrangements and to grieve alongside her mom. The first evening that we were there, after a long day of calling relatives, writing an obituary, making funeral arrangements, and thousands of unbidden tears, I asked Maxine what I could do for her.

"Go to a movie with me," was her reply.

I was dumbfounded. Surely, I had heard her wrong! *A movie? Your dad just died, there are a million things to do, a million tears to cry, and a million memories to savor…and you want to go to a movie?!*

When I responded with an incredulous look, she explained further, "I just need a break from the oppressive sadness. I know a movie won't change anything, but I can't grieve 24/7. I need to go laugh and have some levity in my life. It's like a weighted vest that I just need to take off from time to time and have a respite."

Since then, I have chewed on this spontaneous, grief-stricken wisdom from Maxine. She's right, we can't be assailed by our grief constantly. We will need to consciously take off the weighted vest of grief from time to time. If your child has just come out to you and you are feeling over-whelmed by grief, go on a date with your spouse, go for a weekend away, or buy a ticket to the concert you've always wanted to see. It's true, a significant portion of your life has been affected by your child's revelation, *but not all of it*. Go! Enjoy the parts of your life that are unaltered by this news from your child.

Confide in Friends and Spiritual Advisers

Your third line of defense in your support system is your brothers and sisters in Christ. Some parents feel like they need to tell everyone what's going on with their family when a child comes out to them, while other parents feel like they want to tell no one. There is wisdom in both approaches, but the best answer lies somewhere in the middle.

It wouldn't be wise to tell anyone and everyone this very tender news from your child, especially in the beginning when there are a lot of raw emotions swirling within your family. However, you will need at least two or three trusted spiritual advisers to help you through this difficult time. Make sure you choose wise, discreet, trusted people whom you feel confident can guide you through this righteously and who can protect your family's privacy. See Appendix 4 for an FAQ on determining with whom and how to share this tender news.

Find a Support Group

Perhaps the best resource that anyone in a difficult situation can experience is the support of those who are in a similar situation—people who instinctively know and understand what you're going through, even without you having to say a word. Isn't this the kind of solace and connection we experience within the kingdom of God? Surely this is one of the reasons we're instructed as Christians to not miss meetings of the body: because we need regular connection with those who can deeply and intimately relate to our experiences as we move about as foreigners in this land.[77] You will need the same kind of concentrated connection and perspective as you are navigating life with a child with an LGBTQ+ identity.

I once attended a Narcotics Anonymous support group with my friend, Renee, whose mother was a drug addict. Renee was filled with passion and determination to help save her mother's life by attending this support group. She marched into her first meeting determined to gain concrete tools to make her mom stop doing drugs.

During our first meeting, however, it became very clear that this group was not what Renee envisioned when she signed up to attend. Instead of giving advice on how to get her mom off drugs, the group broadcasted an overwhelming message of personal surrender. Their aim was not to change the drug-addicted family member; it was to help the attending sober family member as they moved through the unimaginable shock, fear, and helplessness.

Though Renee left the meeting in a huff, she has since realized that this was the only power she had in this situation. She did not have the power to stop her mom from using or to take away the pain that the drugs numbed. She only had the power to control her own response, boundaries, and level of surrender surrounding her mother's decisions.

In the same way, support groups for parents of LGBTQ+ children will not be able to offer advice on how to change your child's sexual orientation or gender identity. As parents, we simply do not have control over this. However, these groups can help *you* as you allow your own heart to be refined through surrender and trust. Additionally, these groups can offer practical guidance that other parents have implemented in their own homes, not to change their child's identification, but to set appropriate boundaries within their homes and around how they as parents can help their children navigate their sexual or gender identities.

If you know of other parents in your church or community who have LGBTQ+ children, ask them to get together regularly to vulnerably discuss things unique to your shared experiences. If you do not know of anyone in your local area or do not yet feel comfortable meeting with people in person about this topic, Guy Hammond's Strength in Weakness Ministries has virtual support groups for Christian parents of LGBTQ+

children. These groups have been a lifeline for many Christian parents experiencing a child coming out.

 ## Reflect and Discuss

1. Describe your experience with grief surrounding your child's coming out. What specific expectations are you mourning regarding your child's LGBTQ+ identity?
2. When, where, and how does it feel safest for you to actively grieve and retreat into God?
3. Who makes up your support system and how often do you speak with them about your child's LGBTQ+ identity?
4. What specifically has been difficult in maintaining connection with your spouse during this season?

Chapter 14:

Cultivating a Heart Set Above

My all-time favorite scripture says, "Since, then, you have been raised with Christ, set your hearts on things above, where Christ is, seated at the right hand of God. Set your minds on things above, not on earthly things. For you died, and your life is now hidden with Christ in God" (Colossians 3:1–3).

I can still remember the life-altering perspective shift when I first became a Christian. It was as if I'd been looking through a funhouse mirror my whole life that warped my perspective on reality. When I finally realized who God was and how much he loved me, it felt like someone yanked that funhouse mirror away and suddenly everything seemed clear, in proper perspective, and unadulterated. "I once was blind, but now I see" had never made so much sense to me.

Sometimes, even when we have walked with God for a long time, our vision can become blurred by our emotions, our imperfections, and the distortions of this world. Therefore, we must continually fight for a mindset, a "heartset," and a perspective that is deeply anchored in heaven above.

Respond in Love, Not Fear

If you have had a child come out, you will inevitably camp out in fear for a while. I've seen parents respond with two extremes as they navigate their fear. The temptation is usually to either *withdraw* or *control.* Both are fear responses, and neither is helpful for parents, for children, or for the family overall as they move through this difficult time.

Both fear responses communicate to our children that (1) our love is conditional, (2) we are inherently afraid of them and their actions, and (3) we care about their behavior more than their hearts. None of these are godly perspectives, and they grossly misrepresent what our true hearts should be before our children. Perhaps most devastatingly, these covert messages majorly distort the way our children understand how God feels about them. As God's ambassadors in our children's lives and as the closest example they have of God's love, we *cannot* react in our fear; we *must* respond in love and faith.

God models this perfectly in the way he parents us. We never see God frantically panicking over our mistakes and attempting to control our every move. We never see him withdraw out of fear, unsure and afraid of how to approach us. Instead, we see him get closer in his grief. We see him vulnerably and artfully express his pain and his undying love for us, even when we mess up. We see him gently and wisely persevere, even when we continually run from and reject him. It's true that God has turned his people over to their persistent wanderings before, but it is never done in fear; it is always done in love and surrender.

Fit Those Feet

When I finally came out to my parents in my teenage years, I was surprised, moved, and comforted by their response. Tearfully and terrified, I shared with them that I had previously been in a same-sex relationship and that I experienced attraction to other women. They said, "We know. And we love you."

Though I know not every parent will have the benefit of knowing about their child's LGBTQ+ identity beforehand, having years to process it like my parents did; but, their general attitude of, "We're not afraid. God is above it" was beyond relieving to me as I realized that I no longer needed to manage my parents' reaction (to be sure, this was not their initial *internal* response, and it took them those years of prayer, mourning, and wrestling to get to a place where they could have that external response). Their surrendered frame of heart reassured me that I didn't have to take up the burden of protecting them from me. They weren't afraid of me. They weren't overwhelmed by me. They were securely rooted in the Lord, and nothing was going to shake them.

I've always been struck by the way Ephesians 6:15 talks about having our "feet fitted with the *readiness* that comes from the gospel of *peace*" (emphasis added). No scripture has baffled me more than this one. How could these two seemingly opposing concepts go together? The word "readiness" in this passage brings to mind a battlefield with tensed muscles, all senses on high alert, feet firmly planted, and armored shoes ready to respond to whatever startling ambush awaits around the corner. Yet "peace" brings to mind a "Calgon, take me away" feeling of relaxation where I'm not *ready* for anything except for a nice bubble bath and a good book!

This scripture finally made sense to me, though, when I witnessed my parents' reaction to my coming out. They were not afraid. They were peacefully rooted in the Lord, confident and ready for whatever I was going to throw at them because they knew their role—not to force the compliance of my *behavior*, but to steward my *heart* toward God, even in the midst of my sin, distortion, and pain.

This took a tremendous amount of surrender on my parents' part. They knew that they weren't in charge, but they knew who *was*. That knowledge provided a peaceful readiness as they stepped onto what must have felt like a parenting battlefield—they were serenely prepared to be God's vessels in the fight for my heart.

In order to surrender our fear and respond in our love as parents, we must gain godly perspective. We must perch our hearts in heaven, looking at our child's struggle through the lens of God. I encourage you to take the following steps to set your heart above:

Root Yourself in Truth

Before we can introduce our children to any semblance of truth in some of these difficult discussions, we first must be rooted in the (capital T) Truth of God ourselves.

The Truth is that your child's coming out is *not* your worst fear come true. A lot of parents may feel that way, but it's not. Our worst fear as Christian parents is our children not having a relationship with God. Fortunately, their sexuality or gender identity does not have to hinder that. God's love is much more powerful and intoxicating than who we are attracted to or what gender we most identify with.

The Truth is that our sexual identity and gender identity are *part* of who we are but do not have to take up our entire identity. If God becomes our entire identity, everything else settles in to take up a proportionate amount of who we are and does not have to consume our full sense of self.

The Truth is that we all had adamant, concrete beliefs about ourselves and the world around us when we were teenagers that have come into sharper and more rational focus since then. We need to respect our teens and their view of themselves, but we also need to remember that these proclamations are coming from young minds and hearts that do not yet fully understand who they are. Our children will need some time, grace, and ongoing love to sort this out, just as God affords us.

The Truth is that God is playing the long game for our children's hearts. He is not afraid of their sin. He is not afraid of how long it is taking them to fall in love with him. He is patiently, masterfully, and persistently knocking on the door of their hearts, using everything, even our children's pain and mistakes, to draw them nearer to him.[78]

The Truth is that we all look for fulfillment and identity in things and people other than God. That is not unique to your child; it is simply part of the human condition. Our kids are not engaging in the unthinkable by trying to find contentment in earthly things. *They are lost.* Just like you once were. And they are looking for some comfort and direction in their disorientation, just like you did—just like we were all created to do.

The Truth is that your child's journey to God is not over. They are *on* the path to God, not *at the end of it.* I don't know about you, but my path to God was tumultuous and bumpy! We can't expect that our children's path to God would be any different. In fact, I know that I might never have come to God if I didn't encounter some of those bumps and bruises along the way.

We want to be careful not to stand in the way of a path that may ultimately bring them to God. We must stay rooted in the Truth of God and secure in the fact that he loves our children even more than we do and that he is *always* working.

Consult Your Conscience

After a child comes out, many Christian parents often grapple with concerns such as maintaining harmony in their home, anticipating their child's reactions, and considering perceptions of friends and family. It's important to recognize that, though these are valid considerations, our ultimate aim needs to be higher. The chief consideration for Christian parents in directing their home ought to be aligning their decisions with their conscience before God.

On judgement day, we will have to answer for the decisions we made regarding how we stewarded our children's hearts and how we handled their LGBTQ+ identities. And "I didn't want to deal with their reaction," or "I was worried what my friends and family would think," is not going to cut it. Embracing the commitment to maintain a clear conscience as your guiding principle while navigating LGBTQ+ identities within your home may not necessarily make the journey easy, but it does make it straightforward.

You will have to continually consider various perspectives and factors when managing your household in the context of your child's LGBTQ+

identity. However, anchoring your perspective and decisions in a clear conscience provides a solid framework that promotes peace in decision-making and offers a sense of simplicity, bringing comfort to all members of your family, even if your child may not agree with your choices.

 ## Reflect and Discuss

1. What are your fears as they relate to your child's sexual or gender identity?
2. What biblical truths have you clung to throughout your child's sexual or gender identity journey?
3. What thoughts or scriptures help you maintain a heart set above in your fear?

Chapter 15:

Building Connection Through Effective Communication

S trengthening and nurturing our connection with our LGBTQ+ children is of the utmost importance. Connection—to be known, seen, and understood—is an innate *need* for every human, especially from their parents. As they grow and develop, children will seek connections beyond their immediate family, but this doesn't take away the need for connection to their parents. When their need for connection is not met within the home, children may overly pursue alternative sources of intimacy and connection outside the family. In fact, one thing that can draw people to the LGBTQ+ community is the unconditional love, acceptance, and connection they often experience within it.

Establishing and Maintaining Connection

As our children mature and grow, the ways in which they connect with their parents may change. Become a perpetual student of your child as you adapt to their ever-changing need for connection. The deep, meaningful, and fun connection we cultivate with our LGBTQ+ children can serve as a facilitator for engaging in more challenging conversations. The closeness we build in the parent-child relationship serves as an investment in our overall connection, enabling our relationship to better weather the storms of intense emotions, difficult discussions, and disagreements.

Once our children reach full autonomy and no longer live in our homes, our relationship with them continues, but it takes on a different dynamic. The suggestions in this chapter are meant for parents with children still living in the home; however, these suggestions can serve as foundational guidelines that can be altered to maintain (and forge deeper) connections with your adult child. For further guidance on parenting adult children, see Appendix 4.

I strongly recommend that families establish a dedicated weekly time for individual, intentional connection with their LGBTQ+ child. This time is separate from your family devotionals and should be more intimate, focused only on one child at a time. This time serves as an opportunity to build and strengthen intimacy through bonding, mutual encouragement, and a deeper understanding of each other's lives. It also provides a structured space to address any challenging conversations related to their sexual or gender identity, sparing you from spontaneous, emotionally charged discussions during the rest of the week. Isolating these difficult conversations to this once-a-week time of connection with your LGBTQ+ child fosters a more regulated and emotionally stable environment for such important discussions.

For instance, if your child brings up a sensitive topic during the week, such as their preferred gender pronoun, you don't have to address it immediately. Instead, you can respond with, "I understand this is important to you, and I want to have a meaningful conversation about it. Let's use our special time together later this week to discuss it." This approach allows both of you to acknowledge the issue and prepare for a loving, respectful, and clear conversation, without the pressure of addressing it in the heat of the moment, when emotions are high and rationale may be running low.

Fundamentals of Communication

To maintain strong bonds and constructive communication with our LGBTQ+ children, we must cultivate an environment of openness and vulnerability. From my experience, having the "perfect answer" matters less than ensuring that your child understands three essential things: (1) They are unconditionally loved, no matter what. (2) You are willing to engage in discussions, no matter how challenging they may be. (3) You are committed to navigating this journey together, reassuring them that they are not alone in this experience. Below are some fundamentals of constructive communication to consider as you are engaging in some of these tender conversations with your LGBTQ+ child.

Active Listening. Effective communication starts with active listening. In our Western society, we are trained well to listen in order to *respond*. We are not trained well to listen in order to *understand*. Understanding does not necessarily mean agreeing, acquiescing, or complying. We can understand where someone is coming from while still maintaining boundaries, disagreeing, or declining their requests.

Take it from me, someone who listens to people for a living: I do not possess a superhuman ability to perfectly ascertain someone's experience conveyed in a counseling session. What I do have is practice in being radically present with someone as I seek to understand their experience as thoroughly as possible. "I understand that I don't understand, but I'm here with you" holds greater value than any response driven by listening in order to respond. Active listening is fundamental to building deeper connections and effective communication.

Open-Ended Questions. Open-ended questions seek to draw out the experience of another, thus enhancing communication and promoting active listening. Things like, "Tell me when you first realized you were attracted to the same sex," or "What is it that identifying as another gender would offer you?" We don't just want to understand our child's behavior and thoughts. We want to understand the motivation behind them, the fear underlying them, and the hope they have within them.

Validation. Reflection is a great steppingstone to validation. I refer to it as catching the football. When our kids share their emotions and perspectives, our initial response should be to "catch" their message. We do this by summarizing what we've heard in our own words, thus demonstrating active listening. After reflection, we aim to empathize with their emotions, even if we disagree with their perspective or conclusions.

Christian parents sometimes take exception when I use the term "validation" in this context. I have often heard things like, "I can't validate that my son is a woman!" We don't need to validate the scientific or spiritual implications of our child's LGBTQ+ identity. We do, however, need to validate their emotional experience, even if we disagree with it. For example, "Wow. I can't imagine what it would be like to feel that uncomfortable in your own skin. I'm so sorry you're experiencing this." Reflection and validation are an important investment in effective communication. Usually, our children cannot hear what we have to say unless they first feel seen, heard, and understood by us. Therefore, we catch their football before we throw it back with our own message.

Primary vs. Secondary Emotions. Primary emotions include our delicate and vulnerable feelings such as hurt, fear, and inadequacy. However, these emotions can often feel uncomfortable and even threatening. As a result, we've each developed defensive secondary emotions, like anger, sarcasm, or withdrawal, to shield ourselves from these sensitive primary emotions.

When we express ourselves using secondary emotions, we trigger a secondary emotional response in the person we're speaking to. This, in turn, provokes our counter secondary emotional response, creating a cycle that often draws us further away from resolving the core issue and leads us deeper into conflict. However, when we communicate with our primary emotions—saying, for example, "I'm so hurt" or "I'm so afraid," instead of "I'm so angry" or "How dare you!" we not only convey our feelings but also model vulnerability for our children.

This approach is far more effective in connecting with their hearts than if we mask our tender emotions with a secondary emotional response, which can send the wrong message. Our aim is to communicate openly through primary emotional language and even assist our children in recognizing and expressing their own primary emotions.

Formula for Difficult Conversations

Let's take some of the things we've learned about establishing meaningful connection and fostering effective communication with our children and plug them into an example. Let's say your LGBTQ+ child (a natal female) comes home and asks to wear male clothing. What do you say? Here is a formula you can follow for any difficult conversation or request that your child brings to you:

1. **Clarify:** Repeat back what you heard your child say and make sure you understand their request. Ask any clarifying questions you need to.

   Example: You want to wear men's clothing. What does that mean? You want me to take you shopping in the men's department? You want to dress up in some of your dad's clothes within the house? You want to go to school in men's clothing?

2. **Understand the Underlying Motivation:** Use open-ended questions to draw out the backstory and the underlying motivation for your child. We want to understand why they are requesting this without using the word "why," which can put them on the defensive.

Example: Can you help me understand where this is coming from? What would dressing in men's clothes offer you?

3. **Catch the Football:** Once you have the story and underlying motivation and emotion, repeat it back to your child in your own words and empathize with any primary emotions that you recognize.

Example: Ah, you think that wearing men's clothing will help you hide your breasts, which you feel very uncomfortable with. That would be really tough. I am so sorry you've been feeling that way. I had no idea. We're going to figure this out together, but I just want to say—thank you for trusting me with this experience you're having.

4. **Build in Time to Process:** Once you understand some of the underlying motivations behind their request and you've made a connection with them through validation, it's time to put in a temporal boundary. You will be too emotionally flooded to give your child an answer immediately. You will need time to process your big emotions that are triggered with a request like this. You will also need time to consult your conscience, your spouse, your support system, and God before you can give your child a well-thought-out answer. Make sure to give yourself enough time to process as you clearly communicate when, where, and how you will follow up with your child on this and any boundaries surrounding the time in between.

Example: We know this is really important to you, so we promise that we will pray, discuss, and get advice, and we'll get back to you on this. Because we see this is so important to you and there will be a lot for us to process here, we're going to need some time. So we will get back to you next week during our weekly special time together. Please don't bring it up between now and then, and we promise we will follow up at the appointed time. If you do bring it up between now and then the answer will be an automatic "no."

5. **Follow Up:** Though you may be tempted to ignore it in the hopes that the request will dissipate, it is important to show your LGBTQ+ child that you are a parent of your word. You will also want to show them that you are not afraid of them, their experiences, or their requests. You may not grant them their requests, but you are not afraid of your role as steward in their life.

   Example: Sweetie, last week you asked us if we could take you shopping in the men's department. Thanks for being patient as we processed, discussed, and prayed about this decision.

6. **Set the Boundary Lovingly:** This is the time to give your child the answer you have come to after reflection and consultation with God, your spouse, your spiritual advisers, and your conscience. Keep in mind that this response is not necessarily black and white; "yes" and "no" are not your only options. Because you did the work to understand the underlying desire and motivation your child has in this request, even if you can't give them exactly what they want, you can help them to figure out a way that meets the underlying need or desire while maintaining the boundaries you've set for your child.

   Example 'Yes': We are grateful and honored that you trusted us with this. We can't imagine how difficult it has been for you to feel so uncomfortable in your body. After much discussion and prayer, we've decided to support your choice to wear men's clothing as a means to ease some of your discomfort with your body. It's important for you to know that we believe clothing doesn't define your biological identity. We believe that finding contentment in your identity in Christ is essential, but we acknowledge that you're not there in your relationship with God. Therefore, we respect your autonomy to choose how you'd like to dress at this point in your life.

Example 'No': You know, sweetie, we are grateful and honored that you trusted us with this, and we can't imagine how difficult it has been for you to feel so uncomfortable in your body. We talked and prayed about it, and we cannot in good conscience allow you to wear clothes from the men's section. However, we don't take it lightly that you've been so distressed about your body. We really want to figure out other options that would allow you to be a bit more comfortable in your clothing, but that also fit within our boundaries for you. So we would be happy to buy you a sports bra or a few hoodies that hide your breasts a bit more.

7. **Reevaluate Boundaries as Needed:** Set time intervals to renegotiate this boundary (and other boundaries) you've set for your LGBTQ+ child. I encourage parents to reevaluate boundaries every 3 to 6 months for older children and every year for younger children. Sit down with your spouse during these reevaluation periods and see what needs to be tweaked in your parenting and

in your boundaries for your children. If you decide to change a boundary for your child, communicate it to them clearly.

Example: You know, sweetie, you asked us last year to wear clothes from the men's department and, at that time, we just didn't feel that it was the right decision, though we did get you some hoodies so that you wouldn't feel so uncomfortable in your body. We have continued to pray and get advice about it, and we have decided that, though we don't agree, you are now old enough to make this decision on your own. We ask that in your newfound freedom in this that you respect our faith and our home and don't wear anything too provoking or inappropriate. If you do, we reserve the right to implement boundaries around it while you're living in our home.

Honoring and Connecting with Your Whole Child

Christian parents often find it challenging to envision deep, meaningful connections and healthy, effective communication with their gay or trans child because it may seem like the LGBTQ+ identity looms like a dark cloud over the family. However, this doesn't have to define your reality. Your child's LGBTQ+ identity is just one facet of their experience; it does not encompass their entire being. Approach it accordingly. You can acknowledge your child's gay or transgender identity without letting it dominate your relationship with them or your household.

We certainly don't have to praise or celebrate our child's LGBTQ+ identity, but we also need to show them that we are not afraid of it. As Christian parents, we strive to find that messy middle space between acknowledging and validating our LGBTQ+ children's experiences with their sexual or gender identity and upholding the boundaries we've set within our home for them. Simply engaging in discussions with your child about their LGBTQ+ identity won't reinforce their identification further—but ignoring it might. Clearly communicating boundaries around your child's LGBTQ+ identity won't erase their experiences, but it can provide the structure, stability, connection, and peace that many Christian parents of LGBTQ+ children are desperately seeking.

Make connection with your child one of your prominent guiding principles as you navigate their LGBTQ+ identity with them. Effective communication is very powerful in establishing deep connection—even in the absence of agreement. I meet with a lot of Christian parents who have yielded to their child's demands surrounding their LGBTQ+ identity in the hopes of establishing harmony and connection in their family. However, this approach inadvertently robs our children of the very connection that they (and we) ardently desire.

When we are not transparent with our children regarding our own convictions, principles, and concerns, we hinder their ability to really know us. This is the opposite of what we want with our children—this approach leads to *disconnection.* Wrestling through this together as a family may be difficult and uncomfortable at times, but it has the potential to foster a significantly more profound and more meaningful level of connection with your child.

Reflect and Discuss

1. Describe the typical pattern in your home when you try to address big topics in the moment.
2. What part of the formula for difficult conversations do you find most challenging?
3. How can you validate your child in their LGBTQ+ identity without agreeing?

Chapter 16:

Supporting Mental Health and Weighing Therapy Options

Many parents wonder if therapy is the right answer for their child or family. Therapy can certainly be helpful for any person trying to work through difficult emotions, past experiences, or present perspectives. Family therapy can also be beneficial for families looking to increase their cohesiveness or efficacy in communication.

Goals in Choosing Therapy

Many Christian parents of LGBTQ+ children contact my practice seeking two primary goals: (1) to provide their child with the vital connection they yearn for, and (2) to alter their child's sexual orientation or gender identity. My response to these parents always conveys two crucial realities:

1. Nothing can substitute for the connection of a parent. Therapy can help parents to create and maintain deeper connections within their family, but it is never meant to replace it.

2. Attempting to alter your child's sexual or gender identity is not only unattainable and unnecessary, it is also profoundly damaging. While some individuals may experience fluctuations in their sexual attraction or gender identity, it is not our objective to eliminate these feelings from our child's experience. Rather, our aim is to align their hearts with God's principles, even amid an LGBTQ+ identity.

Achieving this goal does not necessarily require therapy; instead, it calls for the establishment of appropriate boundaries, effective communication, and unwavering love. If you find that you could benefit from honing these qualities, therapy could be a valuable resource for you in learning to do so.

"Should I send my son to therapy because of his transgender identity?" asked a conference attendee. "Does he experience distress over this identity?" I inquired back. "No," answered his mother. "Then he does not need therapy for this. But if *you* experience distress over his identity, then *you* may benefit from therapy." Do not send your child to therapy for something *you* actually need help with.

Therapy can be beneficial for those that are willing to put in the work to get a return. If a child is being forced to go to therapy and is not invested in this endeavor, chances are it will not produce much fruit. You will not only be wasting your money and the time of both the therapist and your child, but this could also frustrate your child, exacerbating connection or communication issues with them even further.

Therapy Approaches

If you have determined that you, your child, or your family would benefit from therapy, you may be wondering what kind of therapist to seek. Christian parents of LGBTQ+ children frequently ask me, "Should I make sure my child only sees a Christian therapist?"

Due to the controversial nature of this subject and to the increasingly litigious society that we live in, many quality therapists are terrified of being sued for malpractice if they do not immediately and unequivocally affirm an individual's sexual or gender identity. Many actively advocate for the client to advance their LGBTQ+ identification further, without considering all the factors or potential underlying reasons. What's even more alarming is that some therapists encourage their clients to vilify anyone in their lives who does not comprehensively agree with or enthusiastically approve of their LGBTQ+ identity.

While I understand the underlying fear for these therapists, this violates the ethical code of every provider. Counselors and therapists cannot ethically impose their own perspectives, beliefs, or ideas on a client. Instead, they are called to look at the situation through the *client's* worldview and walk alongside them while the *client* determines what is best for themselves.

For example, if a client walked into my office and said, "I want to divorce my spouse," the first thing out of my mouth would never be, "Okay, great idea! I think you should do that! Science says there is only one fix to your marital problems and that is divorce. Here are some pamphlets on good divorce attorneys and the divorce process. I expect that by our next appointment you will have reached out to a divorce attorney and started the process."

Instead, any therapist worth their salt would say something to the effect of, "Wow! Okay! What a huge decision you're considering! Let's unpack that a bit. Let's consider the benefits and possible detriments together. Let's walk through your expectations for this and your hopes within it. Let's examine the underlying emotions and desires to ensure this is in line with your beliefs, values, and goals for life," and so on.

To be sure, a therapist ought never to say, "No, I don't think you should do that," or "I think you should do that." It is irrelevant what the therapist's personal opinion is on any matter. Again, an ethical therapist ought to help the *client* determine what is in *the client's* best interest based on *their own* worldview, values, beliefs, and ideas.

If a client holds to a Christian worldview, that ought to be a factor in considering a divorce. Not the only factor, but *a* factor. Similarly, if a Christian client who holds to the biblical sexual ethic tells a therapist, "I'm attracted to the same sex and considering whether or not to pursue a homosexual relationship," the client's faith ought to be a factor of consideration in how to move forward. Not the *only* factor, but *a* factor. Either the client will decide that their faith is central to their identity, even above their sexual orientation, and abide by the biblical sexual ethic, or they will decide that they no longer hold to that belief and change their values accordingly. Either way, the therapist ought to help a client consider all aspects of their worldview in order to maintain ethical practice.

For many therapists, the ethical standard they are held to is compromised when LGBTQ+ topics are brought up. This is what to look out for when seeking a therapist for you, your child, or your family. It's not imperative that you find a Christian therapist; it is imperative that you find an *ethical* therapist who will not be ruled by their own fear or personal opinion on any matter.

Additionally, you need to find a therapist with whom you have a good connection. Studies have shown that the therapeutic alliance is more indicative of positive therapy outcomes than even the theoretical framework of the therapist.[79] If you're able, take time to meet with a few therapists to find the right fit. Just as they will ask you questions on your first session, so you should ask them questions to ensure that you feel comfortable moving forward with that particular therapist. If at any point you feel uncomfortable with a chosen therapist, talk to them about it. Let them know what you're feeling, clear up any miscommunication, and discuss whether a referral to a different therapist might be in your best interest.

Supporting Mental Health

LGBTQ+ individuals experience mental health challenges at an alarmingly high rate.[80] Many parents of LGBTQ+ children are left feeling hopeless, trapped, and confused over how to best support their child's mental health. Seek professional help if you are experiencing this in your home.

As a parent of an LGBTQ+ child with mental health challenges, you will want to better understand your child and the effects of their mental challenges on them and on their gender or sexual identity.

Trauma

Trauma in its very essence *disconnects*. It disrupts our sense of self, safety, reality, and worth. It disconnects our brains from our bodies. And it disconnects us from others. Therefore, the antidote to trauma is not resilience, but *connection*. Because the disconnection that happens following trauma is so pervasive, the reconnection process is often an extensive and even lifelong process. If your child has experienced trauma, pursue professional intervention that allows them a safe and informed place to reprocess their trauma, gaining insights and reconnections to their sense of self, safety, and worth. And then seek professional help for yourself to learn how to best be a support to your child as they progress. Offer your child unconditional acceptance, a "come as you are" approach, as you provide a safe haven of connection for them to tether to in the void of disconnection they are likely navigating.

If you, as the parent, have unhealed trauma from your own past, you will likely be triggered in numerous and unforeseen ways throughout various parts of your child's upbringing. Mental, emotional, and spiritual baggage that we carry as parents creates distortions that end up affecting our children. You have the power to stop the cycle now. Seek professional help to reprocess some of your own trauma. This way you can better connect with them as you steward their heart toward God's perfect lens without passing down warped realities through the generations.

Anxiety and Depression

Many parents of children with both an LGBTQ+ identity and concurrent mood disorders often feel shackled in their parenting out of fear that they will trigger their child's depression or anxiety. We always want to be sensitive to our child's emotional experience, as Scripture tells us not to exasperate them (Ephesians 6:4), but we need not become imprisoned by it. Keep a few things in mind as you are navigating this balance in your home.

Honor their emotional experience, but do not let it rule. Though you may need to be extra empathetic and patient if your child is dealing with depression or anxiety, you also want to make sure that you are maintaining proper boundaries. Recall that boundaries are meant to create *safety* for your child. This is a helpful tenet to always keep at the forefront of your mind as you gear up to implement or enforce a boundary with them. Your child will probably push back—that's a response you can expect. But your child should also expect you to maintain the boundary you've made in your love for them.

Don't punish the depression or anxiety. While we need to maintain proper boundaries and consequences even amid our child's depression or anxiety, we should never punish a child for their depression or anxiety— or shame them for it. I'm not saying we can't uphold boundaries with consequences when our children have depression or anxiety, but we must be sure to set boundaries and consequences around broken rules and family values, not around the depression or anxiety itself.

Separate your child from the experience. It is helpful to externalize your child's depression or anxiety by separating *them* from their *emotional experience*. It's not that your child *is* depressed or anxious—the depression or anxiety is not inherently a part of who they are. Instead, your child is *affected* by depressive or anxious thoughts. It can even be helpful to use this language with your child while empathizing with them or setting boundaries with them.

> **Example:** I see the depression is really affecting you extra hard today, sweetie. How can I help?

> **Example:** It seems like the anxious thoughts are attacking with gusto right now. That must be really tough. I really want to walk alongside you as we unpack those thoughts together, but I cannot allow

you to speak to me like that. When you're able to be respectful, let me know so we can talk through this.

Consider therapy for yourself. If you need help personally in handling your child's depression/anxiety, seek it. Explore whether therapy will offer your child extra help as they are navigating depressive or anxious thoughts.

Suicide and Self-Harm

I can't think of anything that instills panic in the heart of a parent more than a child contemplating suicide or self-harm. This core fear may be triggered every time a parent hears of a young person taking their own life.

For individuals experiencing same-sex attraction or gender dysphoria, thoughts of suicide are not uncommon. Several reliable studies have shown that sexual minority youths struggle with depression and suicidal ideation at a rate much higher than their heterosexual, cisgender peers.[81] Thoughts of suicide or self-harm are not something to take lightly. If your child is suffering from a mental health disorder or thoughts of suicide, make sure to always listen, seek to understand, and get them the help they need.

There is a modern adage often used with parents of transgender children, "Better a live son than a dead daughter." That is, parents are encouraged to give in to their child's identification requests in order to ward off any self-harm or suicide attempts. I don't think there is a parent around that wouldn't agree with that assertion. Preserving the life of a child is one of our most fundamental expectations in parenting. However, allowing our fear to dictate our decisions in parenting is never safe for us or for our children.

Though we need to provide consistent parenting that is not undermined by our child's reaction to a boundary or area of discipline, we also need to tailor our parenting to our specific child based on what's best for them. In that light, if your child is at serious risk of self-harm or suicide, you may need to take drastic measures to ensure their safety.

These drastic measures will look different from family to family, based on the needs and values of your family and the resources available to you. This may include things like inpatient treatment, outpatient treatment, loosening certain boundaries for a time in order to minimize distress, getting your child involved with peers to foster belonging and support, putting extra boundaries around influences that exacerbate the desire for self-harm (electronics, media, peers, etc.), removing items that could be used for self-harm from your child's immediate access, and more. Consider meeting with a mental health professional to discuss ideas specific to your child's needs.

Gabor Mate, a world-renowned author and physician, has said that humans are quite resilient, that we are made to withstand extreme distress and adversity; what we cannot handle is enduring it *alone*.[82] For individuals grappling with the temptation of self-harm or suicide, a profound sense of isolation often intensifies these feelings. Consequently, providing connection, empathy, and compassion through effective communication (as discussed in Chapter 15) is often the most valuable support we can extend to our LGBTQ+ child who is facing such challenges, even if our conscience is unable to agree to all their demands.

The Perpetual Threat

Some teenagers use suicide or self-harm as a threat to get what they want. There may not be actual intention for self-harm; instead, they may be using the threat as a power play. In such a situation, though your fear may be triggered, it will be helpful to focus on the nature of your child as you seek to discern what's really happening underneath the threat. *Never take it lightly or ignore it when your child tells you that they are considering suicide or self-harm.* But if your child has threatened this several times and only when they are seeking to cross a boundary, you may start to recognize a pattern of manipulation.

We do not want to teach our children that we will change our parenting based on their maneuvering. Rather, we want to offer them the same steadiness that God offers us in his heavenly parenting. There is great comfort in God's steadfastness, in knowing that he is the same yesterday, today, and forever, no matter what.[83] We want to offer this same comfort to our children, even when they don't yet appreciate it. In such a situation, it may be helpful to teach your child what a serious assertion self-harm is.

I have spoken with parents who have chosen to allow their child to feel the natural consequences of this kind of manipulative claim. For example, one set of parents whose child frequently threatened suicide as a manipulation tactic chose to show their daughter what it might look like if they sent her to an inpatient facility to get help.

They took everything out of her room that could be used for self-harm, including makeup, clothes, sheets, pills, anything with sharp edges, etc. She had to comply with several wellness checks throughout the day and night. She was subjected to regular drug testing. She was only able to be on electronics and talk to friends with supervision. She had to be up early and go to bed early, ensuring that she got at least eight hours of sleep every night. She had to adhere to a strict schedule and diet. And she was not afforded any privacy, lest she try to harm herself. The door was even taken from her room and replaced with a privacy curtain.

After a few days of this reality, the daughter relented and promised to never threaten suicide or self-harm as a manipulation tactic, only if she was legitimately struggling with the notion. Pray and seek advice from trusted, spiritual advisers and mental health professionals as you seek to discern if your child's assertion is a power play or a real threat of self-harm.

If your child does not have any intention of suicide or self-harm and is engaging in repeated manipulation to get what they want, *it's still a cry for help*. This cry should not be ignored. It could signify a serious issue if your child has to resort to manipulation to be heard.

Seek to understand their experience fully. Validate their emotions and desires, even if you will not allow your child and your home to be ruled by them. Consider getting help through family therapy to build a better connection with your child.

Reflect and Discuss

1. Have you ever gone to therapy? If so, what was helpful or unhelpful about it? If not, what are your thoughts and feelings about pursuing therapy personally?
2. Who or what has influenced your view of therapy?
3. How have you seen your own mental health affect your relationship with your child(ren)?
4. Describe how your child's mental health affects them and the dynamic in your home.

APPENDICES

While you have successfully navigated through the central content of this book, I'm aware that you likely still have many questions. What I do hope I've done thus far is provide you with a framework, a structured perspective, through which to approach LGBTQ+ subjects while remaining anchored to God in the messy middle. Now that you have that framework, we can effectively navigate some frequently asked questions within this discussion. Keep in mind that you will undoubtedly still have questions after reading through these FAQs; it's not my expectation that this book will address all of them. I hope you will be able to extrapolate guiding principles and perspectives offered in this book and in the appendices as you try to find the messy middle in your specific question(s). But before I address these frequently asked questions, I want you to hear the other side of my story—from my parents.

Appendix 1:
A Word from Ellen's Parents

The Story: A Dad's Perspective

Tension hung in the air. Our daughter had just informed us that she was going to move to Florida to live with her grandmother and continue her education online for her sophomore year of college. Unspoken in the haze of emotions, I knew what she was really running away from—a broken heart that she had suffered in a same-sex relationship. And I knew that she felt unable to discuss the truth with us.

We knew she was hurting desperately. I just wanted to hug her and tell her that everything would be okay. Before Ellen informed us about her move to Florida, my wife and I had prayed, talked, received input, and agonized over whether to tell our daughter that we already knew her big, deep, dark "secret."

I strongly believed that, for my daughter in this situation, it was not the time for us to broach the topic. So we impatiently waited a few years for her to initiate the conversation. I knew that I could probably persuade her to stay (which I undoubtedly thought was the best course of action for her) if we could just talk about things and she could open up. But I knew, somehow, that if I pushed, I would be getting in the way of God's plan and my daughter's journey.

In my head, I was crying out, "Noooo, God! Not this way! Not Florida!" Little did I know that Florida was just a steppingstone for our daughter, who would move to Ireland just a year later.

Ellen was a beautiful, feisty, fun, and adventurous child. The moment I saw her, tears instantly appeared in my eyes, and I suddenly realized that this is how God feels about me. My daughter had a heart for and defended the weak. She was a warrior on the soccer fields. She was idealistic, and she loved a challenge.

I knew from an early age that it would have to be a special man who could walk with my daughter in marriage and not feel intimidated and threatened by her. In fifth grade she came home on the first day of school exasperated with many of her classmates and their need to have a boyfriend just to feel good about themselves. I was proud of her but also anguished that, as the years passed, I could see her withdrawing from her friend base because she just didn't seem to fit in seamlessly.

I could see her heart hurting so badly because she was never asked to the dances or out on dates. It pains me tremendously that I didn't know what to say then, that my daughter spiraled into confusion and isolation, and I had no means to fight back other than to love her and pray. I had no idea that she could or would develop romantic feelings toward someone of the same sex.

In Ellen's first year of high school, an older classmate took a positive interest in her. After this young lady went to college, Ellen entered into another friendship with an older classmate, and their relationship quickly went from admiration to almost hero worship. We knew something was "off" about the friendship, but we couldn't quite figure it out.

Months passed, and the situation worsened. Our daughter's moods darkened. We tried to gently have conversations in the hopes that Ellen would open up to us. Though we could talk about some things, she had put a lid on the depths of her heart, blocking us out of a space we were previously welcomed into. The friendship became controlling from both sides and unhealthy.

When the young lady lost interest, Ellen quickly found a replacement for her admiration with a peer classmate. This relationship seemed subtly different from our young daughter looking for validation from the eyes of older classmates. What Ellen was telling us regarding her life and well-being didn't match what we were perceiving. Finally, we secretly read a note in her notebook that was on her nightstand.

> **Stop! We do not necessarily advocate this.** A friend admonished us for this choice. We did not want to snoop. However, we had decided long before to protect our children, even if we needed to protect them from themselves. This was a precedent that we set in our home early on.
>
> For example, when our children got their first cell phones, we told them that they were our phones, as we were the ones paying for them, and it was their privilege to be using them. So we reserved the right to check their phones whenever we felt it was necessary.
>
> The same was true for privacy in their rooms. We made sure not to abuse this power, because we wanted our children to feel safe and have some autonomy over their space and privacy. But when we knew something was up, we would occasionally check our children's phones or rooms to ensure their safety. If memory serves correctly, I believe we checked our daughter's room that one time and our son's room twice.

Learning that Ellen was having a sexual relationship with a classmate who shared her gender at the age of seventeen was incredibly hard to process (remember this was the early 2000s, and it was very different then).

We were shocked, and our initial instinct was to confront her for the truth and details.

But we prayed, and prayed some more, and waited for our emotions to settle and our minds to start functioning again. We were very, very careful about who we spoke with regarding this sensitive topic; we looked for spirituality, love, and discretion in the few people we talked to.

We continued to pray throughout but believed that the best choice was to wait for our daughter to initiate the conversation. Waiting like we did may not be the right approach for every child, but given the nature of our daughter and what we believed was the prompting of the Holy Spirit, we did not bring it up.

This was extremely difficult. The desire to put everything on the table was always pulling at us. We desperately wanted Ellen to turn to God. We also wanted some level of closure emotionally because it was torture to know about her secret but not to be able discuss it with her.

Although she tried to hide everything about her secret life, we could see the subtle changes in her thinking and her more militant posture on cultural things in our society. Her stance on morality began to change. Further exacerbating everything was my perception that the girl Ellen was seeing was dripping with disdain and disrespect toward us. There were times I had to leave the room to pray and settle down because I wanted to remove her from our home.

I kept thinking about Jesus' instructions to turn the other cheek. I kept fervently hoping and praying that our daughter would see our kindness and it would stir her conscience. That didn't happen, at least not within the time frame that I'd hoped.

Every situation is unique. Clearly God (who is always seeking to heal and transform us through love and holiness) guides us each differently, balancing our nature, our past, and our willingness and ability to follow him. It is critical to allow time before a response so that you can settle your emotions and mind and give God's Spirit an opportunity to guide you.

Looking back on this, the two most important things we did were (1) not freak out and react to the situation externally (internally we were a mess and had to continually go to God to surrender this fear and grief) and (2) trust God.

We knew that God loves Ellen even more than we do and that he was diligently trying to reach her heart in ways we couldn't see or imagine. Even though I wanted to fight this battle, as I prayed, I became convinced that God wanted us to sit this one out and allow him to take control.

I wrestle with this even now. We love our daughter and we made sure she knew it all of the time. I understood her desire for older mentors who were also friends, as I had a few of those relationships while growing up. While Ellen was in high school, we had two high schoolers and two toddlers, I ran a business, and we were very busy with church activities.

When we learned about her same-sex relationship, it was very easy to turn the microscope on ourselves and focus on our myriad of shortcomings. The truth of the matter is that our love *could not* begin to approach our daughter's need for the all-encompassing love of our heavenly Father—and that was what Ellen was truly searching for.

The Story: A Mom's Perspective

When our children were very young, one of our biggest concerns was that we wanted to raise them to love God and to decide to follow him one day. This was a little overwhelming because we had already made mistakes as parents, and we knew we were bound to make more. So we went to the Bible and other people of faith for help.

Eventually, we came across this scripture (1 Peter 4:8 NLT) that said, "Love covers a multitude of sins." We thought, "Yes! That's the answer! We know we are going to blow it, but if we love our children and teach them to love, they will be okay." We took great comfort in that. We also knew that if we taught them to love the truth, they would always find their way to God. This is what we prayed for.

The problem is that because of this, I developed some *expectations*—one of which was that my children would accept Jesus as Lord, probably when they were in high school and surely before they left our home. Our oldest son did, and I just knew that our daughter would soon follow. Well, she didn't.

When things in our family didn't go as I had expected, I became full of anxiety and panic. I had this crazy idea that if she didn't choose God when she was young and living at home, she probably never would. I thought, "Well maybe when she's much older and life has beat her down; *maybe* she will turn to God then."

In all my anxiety, there were a few defining moments for me, one of which I treasure in my heart. My anxiety had gotten so great about her not becoming a Christian in the time frame I had expected that my husband had a little discussion with me and tried to talk me down from the cliff.

In that conversation, to my shame, I said these words: "If she doesn't become a disciple before she leaves our home, she never will." And to make it worse, I went on to say, "It's not like anyone raised in church leaves home and becomes a Christian when they're twenty years old!" Guess how old Ellen was when she became a Christian? Yep, twenty. It was like the rooster crowed and the Lord was looking at me with "that look."[84] My anxiety was a result of my incredible lack of faith.

When Ellen got involved in a same-sex relationship, I knew what was happening. I may not have known right away—because I didn't want to believe it. But I eventually knew, even though she didn't come right out and talk to me about it.

At first, I went through all the things we go through as parents. I asked myself, "What did I do wrong?" "Is this my fault?" "Is God letting me down?"

I didn't know if I should confront her, show her what the Bible said about it, or bury my head in the sand and hope it would all blow over. I knew that what Ellen was really searching for was the type of love that only God can offer, but I kept contemplating these fears in my heart: "What if she chooses this path for the rest of her life?" "How will I respond?" "Will I still love her and accept her no matter what?"

I began to realize that nobody could really help me with this. During all that time, I had thought this was all about my daughter and helping her, but now I saw that it had become about *ME*, and I had to resolve some things in my own heart.

I decided to pray, to love, and to honor God as best I could. It was hard. I eventually resolved in my heart that no matter what path my child chose for her life, I would love her and accept her as Jesus would. Not backing down on our beliefs, but loving her in her sin, no matter what.

When she went to Florida, I knew she was searching. I didn't want her to go, but I knew I had to let her go. I didn't know what would happen or how the story would end, but I had this peace that she knew the truth and she would someday return to it.

Surprisingly, I didn't worry that she would be led away from what she was taught. I hated that she was going through this. I always want everything to be easy. This wasn't easy.

The hardest part through all of it was not freaking out over her choices. You know what I mean, parents! I call it the "mommy freak out." It can be ugly, but it's almost a reflex. I had to find inner strength, and I had to trust God.

I had to remember that God loved Ellen more than we did and that this was more about God than about us. In my panic, or my "mommy freak out," I wasn't going to be living out what I always believed in—God's power to overcome and his great mercy. I look back at a time that was very difficult, but it was also a time of us building our faith.

God is truly amazing. It doesn't always come easy, but I'm grateful for the lessons of faith that God allows me to learn even to this day. I'm incredibly grateful to God for eventually giving me what I always dreamed of from the moment my daughter was born—a friendship with her where we share so many things in our hearts and in life, and we enjoy being together.

I'm proud of her, I'm grateful for her in my life, and I deeply respect her. She is an amazing wife and mother and has used her story to help many. God truly is "mighty to save," just not always in the way we expect. This is just our story. I know not every story turns out this way, but faith and love are still required, and the hope we have is never-ending.

Appendix 2:

FAQs: Parenting Through the Developmental Stages

When should I teach my children about sex?

Many parents want to know when to teach their kids about sex (and thus, sexuality and gender). I wish it were as easy as offering a specific point in development. Unfortunately, it is not that simple. There is no specific age that applies to every child. Every child is different, and therefore every child's maturity level is unique. Also, the "right time" depends on you and the values and culture you've instilled in your home. You are the expert on your own family and children. You will need to pray and seek advice to discern when the right time is for *your* child. Keep in mind that this may even vary from child to child within your home. Just because you taught your oldest about sex at five does not mean your youngest will be the same. Be adaptable to meet your child's specific needs. As you are determining when the right time is for your child, here are two things to keep in mind:

Be the first. As much as possible, be the one to teach your child about sex, sexuality, and gender *first,* before they are introduced to their peers' misguided information on such important and delicate topics. Children first learning about sex, sexuality, and gender from their peers or from mainstream media can be extra vulnerable to distortions (lies that we believe as true). Unfortunately, in our modern world, many children are introduced to sexual themes by the time they are in kindergarten. Keep that in mind as you are implementing wisdom to choose the right time to begin these tender discussions with your child.

Not *a* talk, several compounding talks. Teaching your child about sex, sexuality, and gender is not just one conversation. This should be a continuous conversation throughout your child's development. Start with education about the body from birth. Then, when your kids are ready, teach them about sex and the complementarity of the bodies between a husband and a wife. Finally, teach them about biblical gender roles, helping them to sift through earthly gender stereotypes (see Part 3 for more on this). Be intentional about these discussions with your kids. Don't let this be the only topic you discuss with your children, but don't shy away from it either. Allow spontaneous conversations to pop up about sex, sexuality, and gender as well. I've even encouraged parents to utilize TV shows to talk to their kids about LGBTQ+ topics. Be sure to always weave into these discussions the foundational aspects of God's nature, using the formula laid out in Chapter 15.

> **Example:** We watched a show last night where two girls were dating. That might have been confusing to you, because as far as I know, you've never seen that before. What did you think or feel about that?
>
> The truth is that it's not uncommon in our world today for two women or two men to date or get married. This is not what God wants for his people, but God allows us to make these kinds of decisions for ourselves.

> In this family, we believe that romantic relationships should just be between a man and a woman, since that is how God created us to exist. However, we do not look down on, judge, or disrespect anyone that doesn't agree with us or lives a different way.

> It's okay to have different beliefs than other people, and it's okay for people to live differently than we do. The most important thing to be aware of is that God loves them and calls us to love them too, no matter what.

Should I pull my child out of public school?

A lot of very concerned parents have contacted me in recent years about the direction of their local public school and what their child is learning within that environment, especially as it relates to gender, sex, and sexuality. To be sure, some of the things that our kids are learning in our culture both in the school environment and outside it are incredibly alarming. Although I do not think God desires us as Christian parents to walk around in a constant state of hypervigilance to counteract anything ungodly that our children pick up in our world, I do believe we ought to exercise reasonable protections when we can.

One thing we should not do is blame, judge, or look down on other people because they do not live for God. It is ridiculous to expect the world to live the same way Christians do. *We* are the foreigners here. *We* are the exiles. It is not helpful to become enraged and retaliatory when the world does not live according to God's standards. Instead, we can grieve with God, seek to show people his way, and maneuver ourselves and our families within this world in a way that still honors and glorifies God.

Our main goal as parents cannot be to protect our kids from every worldly influence. Not only is this impossible, but it also misses the mark on how God calls us to parent. We are not called to simply shield our children from sin and sinful influences, but to steward their hearts toward God, even in the midst of the influence of sin. We need to use the earthly pulls in their lives to teach and train their hearts how to find God through them.

It's true that school curricula have diverged greatly from what God wants for his people. In some states, it is taught as early as kindergarten that there are more than two genders and that homosexuality is a natural and celebrated form of romantic expression. In other states, high schools allow children to change their name and pronouns to fit their self-perceived gender identity without their parents' consent or knowledge. In some places, high school students leave school to receive cross-sex hormone therapy without the parents even being informed.[85] We are living in a truly unfathomable time. Though we cannot expect the people of this world to live the same way we do, we absolutely can choose what boundaries and protections we put in place for our own children. We can create boundaries that allow our children to reach an age of maturity at which they can handle earthly pulls and influence while simultaneously remaining rooted in a godly perspective.

Although there is no right or wrong answer to the question, "Should I pull my child out of public school?" there is a right and wrong way to go about it. The *what* is not so important here, but the *how* is critical. If you were to keep your child in public school but not talk to them about what they are learning, both from the curriculum and from their peers' influence, this could be detrimental to your child's godly instruction. Similarly, if you were to pull your child out of public school because of the worldly instruction, but not talk to them about matters of sex, sexuality, and gender, this also could be detrimental to their godly instruction.

It matters less whether or not we keep our children in public school (or other areas of earthly influence). It matters much more that we are investing in their godly instruction by transparently, lovingly, and righteously having discussions about some of these difficult topics in our homes. We need to provide a safe, calm oasis to allow our children to unpack the distortions of the world while we compassionately but firmly correct these falsifications.

How do I help my young child who has opposite-sex tendencies?

Many parents experience a low-grade panic if their young child begins to show characteristics more typical of the opposite sex. For example, a young boy likes to play dress-up in his mom's clothes, high heels, and makeup; or a young girl expresses a desire to urinate standing up. If this is something you are experiencing, there are a few things to keep in mind:

1. **Kids are curious.** Not only are kids curious, but they are not bound by the social norms and stigmas that we are (how freeing for them!). We should be careful to cultivate and encourage our children's curiosity while implementing appropriate boundaries around it. It's good for our kids to be curious—that's how God made them! We want them to be delightfully curious in life, always discovering in wonder. Though we may need to implement some boundaries around our children's curiosity, we should always do so in a way that does not create tension or shame around the object of their curiosity.

2. **Could this be a stereotype to confront?** This may be a great opportunity for you to weigh your child's behavior or tendency against God's expectations around masculinity and femininity. It could have less to do with your child and more to do with your own distortions around socially constructed, rigid gender stereotypes.

3. **Do not create shame or tension.** I spoke to a teenager once whose mother was convinced that she was gay because of some of her mannerisms and characteristics. (Side note: Mannerisms and characteristics do not make someone attracted to the same sex.) When I asked the teen if she was attracted to other women, she said, "I never have been, but honestly, because my mom keeps bringing it up, I figure I must be!"

    Sometimes our own fear as parents can create so much tension that we implant experiences into our children's hearts. We need to make sure that we are handling our parental fear in a godly way, striving to see from his perspective and responding to our children in love, so that we do not induce shame into their hearts simply because of our own fear, distortions, and imperfections.

4. **Set appropriate boundaries in love, not fear.** If you determine that a boundary is needed around your child's curiosity or tendencies, then do so lovingly and in a way that does not create shame or tension around the subject. My four-year-old son recently noticed my pedicure and told me how much he loved my "pretty toes!" A few days later, staring at my red toes, he said to me, "Mommy, when I get *my* toes painted, I want to get blue, okay?"

Something like this might induce enough fear in a parent to respond with something like, "What? No! You're a boy, and boys don't get their toes done, only girls do! You don't want to be a girl, do you?!" Instead, in an effort to redirect the conversation to buy myself time to think about how to handle an official request for my son to paint his toenails, I said, "Oh, you like blue better than red, huh?"

When my husband got home that night, we discussed how we would handle it if our son made an official request to paint his toes. We determined that, for our son, this was not a matter of him having a desire to cross God's gender boundaries and present as a girl. This was an innocent, wonder-filled request from an uninformed child who genuinely liked my toenails and had not yet been warped by our culturally constructed gender norms.

We both agreed that, in *that* sense, we had no problem with him putting paint on his toenails. However, because we live in a culture in which painted toenails on a male could lead to certain assumptions about his gender identity, in an effort to be above reproach on this matter, we decided that we would not allow him to paint his toenails.

Though our son has not yet made an official request for painted toenails, my husband and I have already worked out a response if he does. It goes something like this: "You want to paint your toenails because Mommy had hers painted and you really loved them, right? That makes so much sense! But, you know, in our culture painted toenails are mostly associated with women. Though it's not always wrong to paint your toenails if you're a boy, it could be confusing to some people. So, how about instead of painting your toenails, we put stickers on them?"

5. **It is possible.** "Oddly, I feel so relieved you just said that," one mom confessed to me after I told her it was possible that her ten-year-old son may experience persistent gender dysphoria in the future. "Everyone else has assured me that it won't happen, that he'll grow out of it. But there's a part of me that knows this could be a reality for my son in the future too. Ignoring that possibility doesn't take my fear away."

Simply ignoring our fears and assuring ourselves that they are ridiculous and unfounded will do little to comfort us. In fact, ignoring our fears typically only elevates them. It is possible that your young child could experience gender dysphoria now or sometime in the future.

There could be multiple reasons for this gender dysphoria, and there could be infinite ways of expressing it. Seek to understand your child's experience and do not assume they are experiencing gender dysphoria just because they are doing or saying something you do not personally understand. For example, I once had a client call me in a panic because his eight-year-old son was tying his bath towel around his chest instead of his waist. Turns out the son just didn't know that men did not need to cover their chests when getting out of the shower. Unfortunately, the dad's fearful response made this young man feel incredible shame, and he began to wonder if he was fully content in his gender.

Not only do we want to prevent shame and tension around these tender topics for our kids, we also never want to assume we know what their experience is. Instead, we need to seek to *understand* and *draw out* their experience—calmly, not fearfully.

Studies have shown that up to 98 percent of young children with gender dysphoria will outgrow it by the time they reach adulthood.[86] Allow this knowledge to soothe your fearful heart as you watch your child navigate the confusing world of gender expression in our current culture. As with all parts of their development, we cannot expect our children to perfectly understand and execute some of the complex constructs of our world.

Just as we would not expect our two-year-old to run without stumbling or our thirteen-year-old to adhere perfectly to a budget, so we cannot expect our young children to know exactly how to wield their masculinity or femininity. Gender expression is a process that evolves throughout development (and beyond). Let's walk alongside our children as they discover the nuances of their masculinity or femininity.

How do I help my child have healthy same-sex friendships?

Just as romantic relationship has been warped in our modern culture to reflect a be-all and end-all level of importance, so platonic friendship has been similarly warped to depict an enmeshed codependency that offers absolute worth, fulfillment, and identity, especially among young women. These modern depictions are not healthy, and they are certainly not biblical.

We tend to focus a lot more in church culture on *physical* boundaries in relationships than on *emotional* boundaries. I often get calls from parents who say, "My daughter had her arm draped around another girl," or "I saw my daughter kissing another girl," insinuating that *this* is where the impurity began.

Usually, when we dig into the story a bit, we find that the emotional impurity began way before the outward physical display of affection. We need to not only teach our children healthy physical boundaries, but we also need to help them develop healthy *emotional* boundaries in their friendships. This might require us, as the parents, to engage in some reflection on our own emotional boundaries in our friendships.

We must be mindful of idolatry in our friendships and where our fulfillment, identity, and purpose are coming from. Friendship is a sacred, God-ordained construct that serves to give us a different prism of perspective into God's love for us.[87] It is wonderful and ought to be cherished and enjoyed. However, friendship was never meant to replace where God belongs in our hearts—at the *center* of our identity, purpose, and fulfillment.

Just look at Jonathan and David's friendship.[88] They displayed a level of commitment, devotion, and love for each other that would be considered scandalous in our modern culture. But what was at the root of their friendship? God.

Their *connection to each other* did not serve to give their lives meaning or their hearts fulfillment. The *purpose* of their friendship was to draw closer to God through their relationship. Their individual relationships with God provided all the identity, purpose, and fulfillment they needed. Their friendship was the cherry on top, allowing their already filled cup to overflow.

No human is meant to fulfill another human, whether in a platonic friendship or a romantic relationship. This is not a popular opinion in our culture right now. It seems like every TV show or movie would have us believe that another person can complete and fulfill us, make us whole, and can give us all the love we need. Nothing solidifies this earthly perspective more than the iconic 1996 *Jerry Maguire* scene in which Tom Cruise says to Renee Zellweger, "You complete me." Don't even lie—you melted at that scene too! We all swoon over that scene because this is the deepest desire of each of our hearts—to be fully and wholly loved by another. The problem is that the world has convinced us that this is possible with another human, when in reality, it is *only possible with God.* We are constantly disappointed and hurt when we try to fill that God-shaped void in our hearts with human-sized love. It will never fully satisfy.

The first commandment speaks directly to this when God commands his people to have no other gods before him.[89] This means no other source of identity, fulfillment, purpose, or love before him. Let's teach our children the true source of meaning, friendship, and connection, and help them to maintain proper boundaries with their friends, so that they don't blur boundary lines and enter emotional idolatry with a friend that can ultimately lead to physical boundaries being crossed.

It may be necessary to implement boundaries for your child in their same-sex friendships, for a time, until they are at an age of maturity when they can do this for themselves. Consistently point your children to God for their identity, fulfillment, and security. Offer them a deep sense of identity and belonging in your family life as well. Rejoice with them in their friendships and implement proper boundaries around time and influence with their peers to protect their hearts.

What are some resources for teaching my young child about sex, sexuality, and gender?

The best resource you can offer your child as it relates to LGBTQ+ topics is for you, the parent, to better understand God's intent for sex, sexuality, and gender. There are many great resources for this, including *Redeemed Sexuality* by Dr. Jennifer Konzen, *Theology of the Body* by Christopher West, and the Christian Sexuality video series by Preston Sprinkle and Jason Soucinek. There are too many resources for specific situations to list here, but I have compiled a comprehensive list of resources on my website, www.heartsetabove.com, for specific needs related to LGBTQ+ instruction and understanding.

Appendix 3:

FAQs: Sex, Sexuality, and Gender

"Gay" or "same-sex attracted"?

It is becoming increasingly popular for Christians who are abiding by the biblical sexual ethic to identify as *gay* in order to convey which sex or gender they are attracted to. They use this term to identify their experience with their sexuality. I understand this and certainly don't think the use of this term is inherently sinful (though it can be confusing). However, as with anything, there is a chance that sinful desires could underly it. If that is the case, the underlying condition of the heart ought to be the main focus of exhortation, not the external language used.

Personally, my conscience does not allow me to refer to myself as a "gay Christian." Rather, I refer to myself as a Christian who is *same-sex attracted*. This term is accurate in describing my experience without causing ambiguity. For me and my conscience before God, referring to myself as gay would constitute a hint of sexual immorality, as many people might make assumptions about my life and holiness based on that term.

To use a different example, although I enjoy visiting breweries and trying different beers (in moderation), I would not refer to myself as a "bar hopper" or "pub crawler" because those terms may convey a misguided perception about a lifestyle that goes against the central core of my identity, my devotion to God. Similarly, if I were to use the term "gay" to describe my experience with my sexual identity, it could give the wrong impression about my lifestyle. It could suggest that I am living in a way that directly contradicts the most central and foundational part of my identity, Christ.

Therefore, in order to remain above reproach in this area, I use the term "*same-sex attracted*" to communicate my experience with my sexuality. I do not use this term to celebrate this part of my identity as a central and foundational part of who I am. My love for God and devotion to him are far more central and foundational to my identity than my sexual attraction.

However, if your child or loved one is a Christian who abides by the biblical sexual ethic but refers to themselves as gay, I do not personally think this is a hill worth dying on. You may ask your child to consider the implications of their word choice, but ultimately the condition of their heart will determine their righteousness, not necessarily which term they use to describe their experience with sexual attraction.

Why is homosexuality a sin?

Many people who encounter the biblical sexual ethic (especially people who are attracted to the same sex) often ask the question, "But why?" as in, "Why is homosexuality sinful?" I wish I knew! I would really love to understand many of the mysteries and wonders of God, especially this one. Unfortunately, the "why" is not explicitly stated in Scripture.

I trust that if we needed to understand why, God would have made it clear in Scripture. But because he did not make the "why" abundantly clear in Scripture, we must not need that piece of the puzzle in order to obey. Understanding the "why" of something has never been a prerequisite for obedience. In fact, the Bible guarantees that we will most assuredly not understand all the ways of God.[90] The only prerequisite required for obedience is *love*. Jesus says, "If you love me, keep my commands" (John 14:15).

When I tell my four-year-old not to touch the electrical socket, his brain cannot possibly comprehend *why* I prevent him from engaging with something that seems so fun, harmless, and interesting. That's okay. My expectation is not that he will understand; it's that he will trust me—trust that I have his best interest at heart, that I know better than he, and that I would never intentionally bring him harm or unnecessarily withhold anything from him.

In the same way, the theology of sexuality in the Bible is a great opportunity for us to exercise our trust and obedience, even when we don't understand the "why." (Does anyone else have the old hymn, "Trust and Obey" playing in your mind right now?)

Because I have chosen to make God the core of my identity, I have chosen to submit and trust that my Creator knows what's best for me. Living according to God's commands is not a restrictive way of life—on the contrary! This choice allows me to fully submit to the all-knowing love and power of my Creator.

Submitting my sexuality to God's design is not about saying "no" to being with women romantically. It's about saying "yes" to my Creator's intent for my sexuality. I am liberated to experience my sexuality in the way that God intended. I can innocently look up at my Lord and surrender to his protection as I say, "Not my will, but yours be done." Even with my sexuality.

Is same-sex attraction nature or nurture?

In our preoccupied, harried society, we have neglected the spiritual practices of wrestling through difficult concepts with God, sitting in uncertainty and discomfort, and listening to the Spirit. Instead, we have lazily resorted to hastily categorizing difficult nuances of life in order to make cursory, sweeping assumptions before God: nature means it's okay; nurture means it's sinful. Let's *wrestle* with this for a second.

Our culture is obsessed with attributing things to either nature or nurture, as if the answer to that ought to determine whether we abide by God's commands or not. I'm not sure this is the most important question for us to understand as Christians. I am biologically wired to react to everything in anger (shout-out to my fellow eights on the Enneagram!), *and* I grew up in an environment where anger was often portrayed unrighteously. I get this honestly from *both* my nature and nurture influences.

Even so, I know that when I have a fit of rage, I am not acting in congruence with the way God calls me to. When I get to the pearly gates and God and I are discussing my life, I don't think the argument "I was born angry, and therefore I'm absolved of my fits of rage" will hold up. Similarly, I'm not sure that discovering a gay or transgender gene (which has not yet happened) should change the way we view these topics through God's lens.

Don't get me wrong. I certainly understand wanting to fully comprehend God's creation. But if God has not expressly revealed something to us, then we must not need that piece of information in order to obey. God's mysteries, though frustrating at times, are also part of what produces childlike wonder and awe in our hearts as we contemplate our Creator.

As of the writing of this book (2023), science has found no clear and definitive answer to the question of whether our gender and sexual identities are caused by nature or nurture. The best that social scientists can attest to is that gender and sexual identity are influenced by both biology *and* environment. This gives us a great opportunity to exercise our surrender, obedience, and wonder before our heavenly Father.

Although I highly recommend establishing healthy boundaries and protections in your home for your children, it is impossible to undo biology, and it is impossible to protect your children from every single environmental factor that could contribute toward sexual orientation or gender identity. There is not a set list of "nurture factors" that always contribute toward sexual or gender identity. Each person is unique; therefore, each environmental factor in their life will affect them differently and send them on a trajectory completely distinct from anyone else's. This is the beauty of God's creation but also the point of difficult surrender for most parents.

Instead of trying to prevent our child from becoming gay or transgender, let's have our goal for our children rise above our earthly fears and align with God's direction for their lives: to fall so deeply in love with him that they are willing to live and die for him no matter their sexual orientation, no matter their gender identity, *no matter what.*

Are there differences in sexual attraction for men and women?

Male and female sexual attractions have some variation. Sexual attraction for women tends to be more fluid than it is for men.[91] A group of social scientists did a study on sexual attraction and found the following:

> Men are more specific and narrow in their patterns of arousal. That is, heterosexual men are aroused by female sexual stimuli but not male sexual stimuli. For gay men, it's the opposite... Females, on the other hand, whether heterosexual or lesbian, experience arousal to both male and female sexual stimuli, demonstrating a broader, more general pattern of arousal.[92]

This means that, if something has been sexualized, a woman has the potential to be sexually aroused by it, no matter what gender is depicted. This is a huge discovery about female sexuality! Women can be sexually aroused by both men and women. To be clear, this does not assure that every woman will *most certainly* be sexually aroused by any and every sexual stimulus, but just that women have the *potential* to be aroused by anything that has been sexualized.

Consider how confusing this would be for any woman who does not fully comprehend the fluidity of her own sexuality. Imagine a young woman who happens to see an overly sexualized commercial of another woman, feels sexual arousal over it (an automatic response that she has no control over), and does not understand that her arousal may not be because of the gender portrayed but simply because that content has been sexualized. In today's progressive climate, that alone may be enough to convince a young woman that she is gay, simply because she experienced sexual arousal toward another female—which is something that's not uncommon, even for heterosexual women.

Understand the Differences: Breadth

Not only is female sexual attraction more fluid than male sexual attraction, but it's also broader. Dr. Lisa Diamond, a lesbian psychologist studying female sexuality, did a ten-year longitudinal study on female sexual identification and found that,

> Among women who initially identified themselves as heterosexual, lesbian, bisexual, or "unlabeled," after ten years, more than two-thirds of the women had changed their identity label a few times. When women changed their identities, they typically broadened rather than narrowed their potential range of attractions and relationships.[93]

Over the course of a woman's life, it is not uncommon for her to ascribe to multiple sexual orientations. It's not that women are constantly changing whom they are attracted to, but the range of potential attraction is broader for a woman compared to that of a man. If society insists on placing all these descriptors on sexual attraction (i.e., gay, straight, bisexual, pansexual, etc.), then some women may appear as if they are changing who they are attracted to constantly because their attraction ability exists in such a wide range.

Social scientists have also found that, generally, women and men connect differently.[94] Women usually won't want to physically connect with their partners until they first feel emotionally connected to them. Men tend toward the opposite approach. Usually, men's emotional connection to their partners is propelled by a physical connection.

It makes sense, then, that a woman's attraction has the potential to develop toward whomever she feels emotionally connected to. During the prime time that sexual orientation develops, the adolescent years, to whom do preteen and teenage girls usually feel most connected? Usually, it's their female peers. And the crux of that desire for connection typically has little to do with a physical connection; it's rooted in emotional connection and intimacy.

So we can see how easy it is, especially for young women, to unexpectedly end up in a same-sex relationship that started innocently with an emotional connection. We need to be discussing these things with our kids and normalizing their desire to want to belong and connect deeply with their same-sex peers while pointing them to the ultimate source of connection and intimacy: God.

Understand the Differences: Milestones

While sexual orientation is developing throughout childhood and early adolescence, both men and women experience certain milestones in that development.[95] One of the most fascinating pieces of research that I've come across says that men, when they are about twelve or thirteen, usually know which gender they're attracted to, though they usually have not expressed it to anyone by then.[96]

Women, on the other hand, are typically not rooted in their sexual orientation until they are about fifteen years old.[97] This means that young women have two or more extra years of being influenced by all the environmental factors that could contribute toward sexual orientation development (culture, early exposure to sexual elements, family dynamics, personal insecurities, trauma, etc.).

What makes this even more alarming is that a major environmental factor in sexual orientation development is an individual's first sexual experience, which happens within the adolescent age range for many. If a young person has their first sexual experience with someone of the same sex, their brain will create neural circuitry that lays the foundation for future sexual connection. They may form a strong association with this first experience, intertwining the concepts of sex, sexuality, romance, love, and intimacy with individuals of the same sex.

I've talked to too many women who thought that it was harmless to "experiment" with their female peers in a sexual way as a teenager only to find out that, later in life, they have a problem connecting deeply with their husbands because their brain is expecting something similar to their first sexual experience. I am living proof that God is bigger than an individual's first sexual experience, but our children ought to be informed of the dangers of "experimenting"—it's not as harmless as our culture makes it out to be.

Can sexual orientation change?

I want to be careful how I answer this question, as some people have twisted the premise of sexual fluidity in order to sanction reparative therapy. *Reparative therapy*, or conversion therapy, is an outdated, harmful, widely discredited, and often illegal practice that seeks to change someone's sexual orientation. To be clear, there is nothing in the Bible that states that being *attracted* to the same sex is sinful; therefore, reparative therapy is not just harmful, it is completely unnecessary.

This destructive method has not only been the source of overwhelming psychological, emotional, and spiritual pain, it has also caused people within God's kingdom who do not have a heterosexual orientation to feel as if they are outcasts, unworthy, and inherently shameful.

As of now, science has determined that sexual orientation is not an innate trait like eye color.[98] Rather, sexual orientation is a combination of both biological (nature) and environmental (nurture) factors. We are all born with certain biological predispositions. Throughout the course of our development, different life factors influence these biological propensities and send us on a unique trajectory distinct from anyone else's. Perhaps a good parallel trait with which to compare this would be humor.

It could be argued that humor, like sexual orientation, has a biological component to it as well as an environmental component. So, can humor change? Somewhat. If you're asking if Jerry Seinfeld could ever be mistaken for Adam Sandler in humor style, then no. But I am sure that Jerry Seinfeld's humor has developed and morphed over his many years of honing it, including being influenced by the people in his life and in his field, his varied life experiences, and the influence of different aspects of our society.

Similarly, sexual orientation in an individual cannot do a 180-degree flip, but for some, it can experience some fluctuation along the continuum, based on the person's unique biological factors and life experiences. Sexual orientation develops throughout our preadolescent and adolescent years. Like humor (and other non-innate traits), it can fluctuate for some people. It is subject to influence from the society we live in, the people we surround ourselves with, what we watch on television, and our exposure to social media, pornography, traumatic experiences, and so on.

Dr. Lisa Diamond, one of the leading experts on sexual fluidity, has found that variability in sexual attraction exists for both men and women. Though sexual fluidity is more common in women, there is substantial evidence that some men also experience variability in their sexual attractions.[99] In fact, bisexual attractions are more common than exclusively homosexual attractions for both men and women.[100]

So, can sexual orientation change? For some people, variability in sexual attraction does exist. For other people, it does not.

Perhaps a more important question is: Should we try to change our sexual orientation? No. This could be futile and harmful. If our goal is holiness, who cares what our sexual orientation is? Perhaps your sexual attraction will experience variability, perhaps it will not. Either way, our target remains the same: holiness.

Is being asexual wrong?

Asexuality, or the lack of sexual attraction, is not inherently sinful. We all have distinct patterns of attraction and libidos. Just because someone may experience a lower libido or desire for sexual connection does not mean it is pathological or sinful. In fact, someone who experiences a lower threshold for sexual attraction may be better equipped to experience the joys and gifts of celibacy.

Just as with any pattern of sexual attraction (or lack thereof), it is a neutral reality—not inherently sinful or righteous. It is what we *do* with that pattern of attraction (or lack thereof) that can determine who we will serve with it—God or ourselves. For instance, a Christian who feels minimal to no romantic or sexual attraction to others would still need to aim for deep, meaningful intimacy with both God and others. Likewise, if a Christian identifying as asexual were to prioritize their earthly label of "asexual" over the core aspect of their identity, Christ, it would constitute idolatry, and therefore become sinful. If this were to happen with a fellow sibling in the faith, it should be the idolatry that is challenged, not the lack of attraction toward others.

I do want to put a special note in here about trauma. Those who have experienced trauma, especially sexual trauma, may have a reduced desire for romantic or sexual connection as a result of that trauma. This is still not sinful, but it is worthy of extra care and compassion. It should be noted that not everyone who experiences asexuality most certainly has a trauma history; and not everyone with a trauma history will experience asexuality. But if someone does have a trauma history and experiences asexuality, the focus should be on helping that individual to reprocess and heal from that trauma, not to restore or cultivate their sexual attraction.

Can gender change?

There are three levels of transformation for those who seek to exist within a different *gender identity*. The first and least invasive level of transition is *identification*. This means that anyone experiencing gender dysphoria or incongruence can identify as the opposite gender, nonbinary, or nongendered through the use of different clothing, pronouns, names, etc.

The second level of transition is *hormonal intervention*. This is when a person undergoes cross-sex hormone therapy by receiving inordinate amounts of hormones that are correlated with the opposite sex. That is, natal males receive high amounts of estrogen or progesterone, and natal females receive high amounts of testosterone in order to produce secondary sex characteristics correlated with the opposite sex. Natal females who take cross-sex hormones often experience changes such as facial hair growth, a widening of their face, a body shape that is less curvy, and a deepening of their voice. Natal males who receive hormone therapy treatment may gain some softness in their features, particularly in their face and chest. Their voices may become higher in pitch, and they may stop growing facial hair.[101]

The third and most invasive level of transition is *surgical intervention*. This could involve a series of multistep procedures, for both men and women, to remove the primary sex characteristics (e.g., penis, vagina, breasts) in order to create genitalia and other primary sex characteristics correlated with the opposite sex.

Some people within the LGBTQ+ community (and beyond) correctly assert that these levels of intervention allow one to become a *trans* man or a *trans* woman. That is, they still belong to the category of their natal sex, but they have altered their identity, hormones, or genitals to correlate with the opposite sex. Others in the LGBTQ+ community (and beyond) believe these levels of transition constitute a *literal* shift in natal sex, thus correcting a *felt* reality through biological intervention.

Modern science is a marvel capable of many things. However, sex (aka gender) is a biological fact that cannot be altered. Although a person can alter their *gender identity* by changing their name, pronouns, hormones, and even their genitals, one cannot alter their gender. Gender is not just skin deep; it is woven into our chromosomes, our DNA, even our very bones![102] These fundamental, structural, and *unalterable* parts of self all point to the gender binary that God intentionally created. Gender is not just a social construct; it is a biological fact and a theological wonder that cannot be altered by humans.

What about eunuchs?

Queer theology will often point to eunuchs as proof that God never intended for gender to exist in a binary, especially since Jesus refers to eunuchs in a positive way in Matthew 19. I cannot make sense of this claim at all. "Eunuch" was a term used in ancient times to describe a biological male who did not have testicles. Whether he was born that way, made that way, or chose to become that way,[103] the term "eunuch" was not used to denote a person of a different gender, as though the eunuch were not a *man*; rather, a eunuch was a *type* of man. Therefore, eunuchs exist within the gender binary that God created.[104]

There certainly would have been some nuanced complexities to living as a eunuch in the kind of patriarchal society that existed during Jesus' time. Damaged testicles would have significantly impacted a man's standing; for example, his ability to procreate and his testosterone levels, which in turn might have affected his stereotypical masculine traits, like a deep voice, hair on the body, or aggression.

Certainly, a tremendous amount of compassion and understanding should be exhibited toward someone living outside the cultural, stereotypical gender norm. We also need to be continually confronting these gender stereotypes in our own hearts to ensure that we are holding to God's standards of masculinity and femininity, not distorted earthly stereotypes. That way, people living outside the cultural norm do not feel inherently sinful simply because they lack an *earthly* ideal. However, Jesus mentioning eunuchs in the Bible in no way negates the gender binary that God created.[105]

What is the truth about transgender identities?

During my recent encounters with two different medical providers regarding a health concern, they provided conflicting recommendations. This left me deeply frustrated and anxious as I grappled with deciding which guidance to follow. In the midst of this inner turmoil, I had an epiphany: My experience with these medical experts mirrors the frustration and anxiety induced by the deluge of conflicting headlines, soundbites, and statistics we encounter every day regarding transgender identities. It's not an uncommon occurrence to come across headlines that span from "Changing Genders Could Jeopardize Your Life!" to "Changing Genders Could Save Your Life!" within a single day. The exasperated question often arises, "What is the truth?"

The truth is that the truth is hard to determine right now. The current lack of substantial, long-term data hinders our ability to fully grasp the implications of transgender identities for both physical and mental well-being. In fact, a comprehensive understanding of the repercussions of contemporary gender perspectives is at least a decade away.

In her book, *The End of Gender*, Dr. Debra Soh, a distinguished neuroscientist, sexologist, and researcher, reveals the current challenges associated with acquiring reliable and impartial data within this domain. Soh, a non-Christian, liberal scholar, has experienced firsthand the consequences of being canceled due to publishing substantiated research that contradicts the agenda of transgender activists. She portrays a vivid depiction of academic individuals who, despite conducting rigorous research, find themselves hesitant to publish their findings due to the potential repercussions in today's society. This contemporary culture's aim does not seem to be merely discrediting flawed research, but rather actively working to undermine and silence anyone who dares to publish results that oppose the objectives of activists, regardless of the veracity of their reports.

At this stage, a couple of certainties have emerged, but the underlying reasons are still not clear. For example, we know that transgender individuals are four times as likely to struggle with mental health conditions,[106] but we don't know why. Is the mental health struggle among trans individuals a result of the significant societal stress and challenges faced by those with an LGBTQ+ background, or are they turning to gender nonconformity in order to cope with their mental health struggles? Research has yet to provide a conclusive answer.

There are many unknowns, even in the certainties that have come to light in the data. For instance, consider that transgender individuals exhibit a suicide risk twenty times higher after transitioning,[107] yet the reasons behind this trend are not clear. Similarly, though we know that long-term cross-sex hormone therapy's effects are not completely reversible and can lead to many dangerous side effects, the complete range of potential long-term side effects and possible remissions remains unclear.[108]

Unfortunately, misinformation permeates in all directions in the contentious subject of transgender identities. Exercise caution toward those who assert absolute certainty in any of these areas. Should you encounter claims declaring transitioning as the sole path, devoid of risks—exercise caution. Likewise, if you hear claims that transitioning will inevitably result in fatal consequences—exercise caution. The current shortage of dependable data and substantial evidence leaves a great deal unsettled within this domain.

Rather than seeking absolute certainties in such a complex realm, surround yourself with individuals and materials that honor the messy middle—a nuanced space where humility and faith intersect. I've compiled a roster of individuals and references on my website, www.heartsetabove.com, that excel at embracing this approach. Fortunately, God has relieved us of having to determine absolute truths—that is his job. We are simply called to love him and love others, even in the midst of all the unknowns.

Appendix 4:

FAQs: Parenting LGBTQ+ Children

Do my child's values have to be the same as mine?

When our children are young, their values are our values because they are not yet able to think for themselves in this way. When our children are adults, our values are not necessarily their values, because they are able to think for themselves and live by their own values. Adolescence is the chaos that bridges these two realities.

There is usually a *gradual* shift between imposing our values on our children in their youth and emancipating them from our values in their adulthood. This doesn't happen overnight, but slowly throughout their preteen or teen years as we give them more and more age-appropriate autonomy and freedom. Because this gradual shift depends on a child's age, maturity level, and emotional intelligence, it will look different from family to family and even from child to child. Only you can determine whether your child should still be held to certain values you have that they may not share.

For example, when I was fifteen, I wanted to stop going to church, but my parents felt that I was not yet able to make that decision on my own and that I still needed to adhere to our family values as they related to church attendance. So I continued to attend with them. When I was seventeen, I asked my parents to reconsider. They determined that, though they did not agree with my decision, I was then old enough and mature enough to make that choice for myself. Therefore, it might be appropriate to set a boundary for a certain time in your child's life and renegotiate it as needed as they mature.

How do I accept my child without affirming their LGBTQ+ identity?

Acceptance is rooted in surrender, which is always accompanied by grief. Grieving our lack of control over our children's lives and hearts is a continual, lifelong process every parent would do well to get comfortable with sooner rather than later. We can wholeheartedly accept the truth that our child has the God-given free will to live their life however they would like to. We can also accept them for who they are, without condition, just as God does with every human. When we accept them in this way, we convey that we love our children unconditionally, just as God does with each of us. Our love for our children is not dependent on complete agreement with them, just as God's love for us is not dependent on our absolute understanding of and agreement with him.

Affirmation insinuates approval. Though we may not be able to approve of or affirm every decision our child makes in life (LGBTQ+ related or not), we can absolutely still accept them—both their free will and them as a person that we love wholeheartedly without reservation, all the while maintaining connection with them no matter what.

Could an LGBTQ+ identity be a phase for my child?

Though it's never helpful to have a fear-based reaction to our child's LGBTQ+ identity by proclaiming to them, "It's a phase! You'll get over it!" it is good for parents to keep in mind that as preteens and teens explore life, there will be lots of changing aspects in their identity throughout their development. An LGBTQ+ identity could be one of those aspects that change—or not.

In my teenage years, I had a unique experience among my peers because I witnessed my parents raising young children. My parents had a surprise child when I was twelve and another when I was fourteen (to which my response was, "Again?! You know how this works, right?!").

By the time I was fifteen years old, after three years of witnessing the chaos and upheaval that children can bring to a home, while lacking the understanding of the joy that children can bring, I emphatically declared, "I will never have children!"

My parents (and other trusted adults in my life) assured me that this concrete, teenage conviction of mine might not last all the way through adulthood, but I vehemently disagreed and protested, "I promise, you wait and see, I will never have kids!" Now, as I listen to my four-year-old playing in the other room and as I feel my unborn child move around in my pregnant belly, I can't help but chuckle at my teenage shortsightedness.

While teenagers may wholeheartedly believe their emphatic declarations in that moment, these are not infallible predictions of how their lives will eventually turn out. It is helpful for parents of preteens and teens to remember this and not get swept up in the fear of their children's "definitive" proclamations. We can still validate their experiences and emotions while keeping in mind that things could change as their brains continue to grow and mature.

However, it is always a possibility that our children's LGBTQ+ identities will persist beyond adolescence into adulthood. Parents of LGBTQ+ children ought to be continually moving toward a surrendered heart before God so that they are prepared for this possibility. It is never wise to pause our internal refinement generated by a child's LGBTQ+ identity in the hopes that it's a phase and will all blow over. When we freeze in our fear like this, we not only rob our children of deep connection with us in the midst of their LGBTQ+ identity, but we also rob ourselves of all the spiritual fruit that can come from wrestling in our hearts through this time and being extra reliant on God.

How do I determine whom to tell about my child's LGBTQ+ identity?

I had a spiritual leader once who, with head tilted and slightly raised eyebrows, said to me, "You know how the church is!" referencing how much gossip can be present in the body of Christ. Yes, we all know how the church can be. When your child comes out, it is not the time to dole out this very delicate information and subject our children or families to gossip, ridicule, or unsolicited opinion. However, we will absolutely need outside help when we are navigating something like this in our homes.

When I was eight years old, I got caught kissing a boy. My parents were shocked, grieved, and terrified. I was embarrassed and ashamed. After they comforted me in my own poor decision-making, they let me know there would be consequences, but that they would need to get advice first. They assured me that they were not going to announce this news to the world, but instead gave me the names of the two people they would talk to in order to get some guidance.

They settled my shame-filled heart by letting me know their reason for getting advice: "Honey, we're going to get advice on this for *us* to get the help that *we* need. We're not perfect parents, and we're still learning how to be the best parents we can possibly be for you. God says that we can't do that alone and that we need the help of other people to love you the best that we can. That's why we're going to talk to these two people—not to talk about you, but to get help for us."

After they spoke with these two trusted spiritual advisers, they communicated the consequences to me and assured me that the two people they talked to had reiterated their love for me and for our family when they spoke. The next time I saw those two people in the fellowship at church, they each came up to me and gave me a big hug. They didn't mention anything about my indiscretion or their conversation with my parents, but they made sure I knew that I was loved by them. Though this process certainly didn't feel comfortable at the time (I still begged my parents not to tell anyone), I was offered a deep sense of security through my parents' transparency with me and through the careful consideration they gave in whom to trust with this information.

This is a great depiction of how to navigate something as sensitive and delicate as LGBTQ+ identifications coming up in your home. As a child, instead of spiraling in insecurity every time I walked into our church building, wondering whom my parents had gotten advice from, convinced that every glance in my direction or every lowered voice that I passed was about me, I felt a sense of security in knowing exactly who my parents had talked to and their reaction.

And instead of my parents having to navigate this alone or feel as if they needed to lie to me about talking to other people, they were able to confidently navigate this righteously and transparently, getting the help they needed but still protecting my privacy. We can get the help we need as parents, all while modeling our humility before our kids and assuring them of our commitment to protect them in their experiences.

How do I tell my other children about my child's LGBTQ+ identity?

An LGBTQ+ identity can create a lot of tension within a Christian home. This tension can often be very present with siblings of the LGBTQ+ child. This does not have to be the case. All of your children will look to *you* to provide the stability, boundaries, and peaceful rootedness (see Chapter 14) for any major turbulence within your home, including around LGBTQ+ identities.

As with any difficult conversation you have with your kids, it matters less *what* you say, it matters more *how* you say it. Be sure that you have put in the work to set your heart above in your perspective, so that you are able to allow love, humility, grace, peace, and faith to overflow from your heart and out of your mouth as you discuss this with your other children.

You will first need to determine whether this is a conversation you would like to have as a family (with your LGBTQ+ child present) or individually with your other child(ren). It may be good to have a one-on-one conversation with your other child first, but schedule a follow-up family conversation about it so that transparency and connection can permeate the whole family. Be sure to give yourself and your other child enough time to process before you have this conversation as a whole family, with your LGBTQ+ child present.

You can modify the formula laid out in Chapter 6 to discuss your child's LGBTQ+ identity with your other child(ren), first explaining it through an earthly lens, then explaining it through a godly lens. Then allow space for them to have an emotional response to this news (even if it's not in that moment, you can have a follow-up conversation after they have had time to process). You may want to help provide clarity and structure for them by informing them of the boundaries you've implemented for your LGBTQ+ child. Finally, help your other child(ren) come up with a plan for processing this information and for interacting with their LGBTQ+ sibling.

> **Example:** Sweetie, I wanted to make sure that we touched base together about your sister's LGBTQ+ identity. She has just come out to us as transgender. That is, she feels as if she identifies more with being a male (*explaining it through an earthly lens*).
>
> We hurt for her at the distress she's feeling in her femininity. But, because we live for God, we do not believe this is the best way for her to handle this distress. However, we want to help your sister as much as we can in this immense distress she is feeling (*explaining it through a godly lens*).

I know this is some big news; how are you feeling about this? If you don't know right now, that's okay, we can check back with you this weekend during our regularly scheduled time of connection (*allowing space to respond emotionally*).

Can you imagine what it would be like to feel so uncomfortable in your very body? What have you noticed in your sister that we need to be aware of? (*cultivating empathy and compassion*).

We have decided that we will still refer to your sister as "she," but we have agreed to call her by her pre-ferred gender-neutral name (*informing of boundaries implemented in the home*).

What do you feel comfortable with calling your sis-ter? What are some ways that you think you would like to honor your sister and her experience, but still remain within your own conscience and boundaries with this? (*making a plan*).

What if my spouse and I disagree?

"My husband doesn't even want to talk about it; he's still in denial. I feel so lonely." These were the tearful words from a mom I met at a sem-inar. Having your child identify as part of the LGBTQ+ community can be a scary and grief-filled time for many Christian parents. It is likely that you and your spouse may be in different places emotionally as you process your grief and fear.

It is also common for Christian parents to disagree on some decisions surrounding their LGBTQ+ child's identity. One couple recently told me that they didn't agree on what to call their child. The mom's conscience allowed for her to call her daughter by he/him pronouns, but the dad's did not. This is to be expected as well. There are lots of subtle decisions that will need to be made as you are setting up boundaries within your home around your child's LGBTQ+ identity. It is likely that you and your spouse will not agree on every single one of them.

Whether you are dealing with disagreement or different stages of processing, allow some space for your spouse to wrestle through this and to grieve, mourn, and retreat into God for a time. Usually one spouse moves a bit quicker in terms of emotional processing than the other. Make sure to allow time for your spouse to move through some of these big emotions and don't make them feel as if you've left them in the dust. Ask if you can share with them what you're feeling without expecting them to reciprocate as they get their bearings.

> **Example:** I know you might not be ready to talk about this yet, but would you be willing to listen? I've been processing it and would really love to share with you what I'm feeling. I won't expect you to reciprocate with what you're feeling just yet, because I know you're still processing, and I want to honor that. I do ask that you are gentle with me while I'm sharing and that you let me know you heard me.

Make sure that you make yourself available to your spouse if they take a bit more time to process. Actively listen to what they share and reflect back to them what you heard them say so that they know you are trying to understand the depths of their heart in this.

> **Example:** Honey, I want to understand how you're feeling and what you're thinking about this, but I'm unable to share what I'm feeling at the moment because I'm still processing. I promise that I will let you know when I'm ready to share with you. Until

then, I would love to seek to understand how you're
feeling in all of this.

Be sure to also spend time connecting to your spouse in other ways. Your child's LGBTQ+ identity should not be the only topic of discussion in your relationship. Though it is an important thing happening in your family, it is not the *most* important thing. Treat it as such, and do not let it dominate. Take extra measures to connect to your spouse during this difficult time. Take a weekend away, go out for a few hours without the kids, or lock yourselves in your room to block out the noise of the world for a bit. Remember that your connection with your spouse is much more than your shared duty in parenting. Indulge in that connection!

Should I allow my gay child to date?

It can feel completely overwhelming to determine some of these boundaries within your home. Before you get down to the nitty-gritty of the boundaries you want to implement around same-sex dating, you may want to first spend some time thinking through your beliefs on the purpose of dating. Some Christian parents have told me, "The purpose of dating is to determine who you will marry. Because we do not believe same-sex marriage is what God wants for his people, we cannot allow our child to date someone of the same sex." There is merit in that view.

Other Christian parents have told me, "Dating at a young age exists to grow socially and to learn about the nuances of romantic relationships while you still have the protection and oversight of parents. Therefore, we can consider allowing our child to date someone of the same sex, if they will abide by the rules and boundaries we set around it." There is merit in that view as well. Set your own framework for why dating exists before you determine what boundaries need to be set around it in your home.

If you've determined that what you believe about the purpose of dating permits you to allow your child to date someone of the same sex, then you may want to consider what the general rules around dating are in your home. You may want to set aside the same-sex element for a moment as you determine whether your child is ready to date at all. Are they at an age and maturity level where they can be in a romantic relationship—no matter what gender is involved? If your child is allowed to date in general, what rules would be involved if they were dating a person of the opposite sex?

Here are some examples of dating boundaries some Christian parents have implemented for their kids:

❖ Parents need to meet the significant other first.

❖ No kissing.

❖ The kids can't be alone together.

❖ They can't talk past 9:00 p.m.

❖ They must limit time together, not becoming consumed with their relationship.

❖ The couple must spend time with each other's families together, etc.

If you determine that you will allow your child to date someone of the same sex, make sure you're consistent with your boundaries around dating. You may need to implement a few boundaries specific to same-sex relationships as well (e.g., no sleepovers). Be sure to renegotiate boundaries regularly and communicate them if and when they change.

What if my child is an adult?

While adjustments may be necessary to accommodate your child's full independence, the guiding principles in this book remain applicable when parenting an adult child. As our children achieve complete autonomy and leave our homes, the connection we've cultivated throughout their lifetime endures, albeit in a different form. Although this phase with your child can feel intimidating and emotional, remember that their autonomy is a positive and God-given aspect (see Chapter 4).

In fact, their autonomy can enhance your relationship! Your role no longer involves directing their spiritual journey, teaching them what and how to think, or molding their character. Those chapters in your relationship with them have concluded. While you may reflect on past decisions with some regret, it's essential to accept that, though you did not parent perfectly, you did the best you could with the knowledge, maturity, and resources available to you at the time. Let this realization ease your grief, guilt, or shame as you concentrate your efforts on the present, seeking to build a deeper connection with your adult child. Here are some reminders as you're navigating your adult child's LGBTQ+ identity:

Extra Surrender. Though all of the guiding principles in this book apply, as a Christian parent of an adult child (LGBTQ+ or not), you may need to add an extra dash of surrender to the equation in order to honor the autonomy that your child has.

Model Authentic Discipleship. Though you no longer have authority over your child, you do still have *influence* over them. One of the most effective ways you can exert that influence is by exemplifying authentic discipleship. I'm not talking about feigning perfection to project an image of righteousness. Instead, I'm referring to *genuine* faith—messy as it is. Let love cover over as you wrestle through your imperfections toward the messy middle—where the perfect balance of love and righteousness reigns. Allow your child to witness your struggles, failures, repentance, and perseverance. Your role may no longer be to actively steward your child's heart toward God, but you can still light the path for them by modeling a surrendered, humble, and faithful, albeit imperfect, life for them to observe. And God can do immeasurably more with your imperfect example.

Connect Deeply. Perhaps a parent's main goal in their relationship with their adult children is to establish, maintain, and deepen connection with them—even if there is disagreement. Remember, we don't need to approve of every decision our child makes in order to accept them just as they are. Focus on creating positive times of connection with your adult child so that there are regular deposits going into the "connection bank," which may help mitigate the effects of inevitable negative interactions. What your adult child wants more than anything from you is unconditional love and respect.

See *All* of Them. Your adult child's LGBTQ+ identity is part of who they are, not all of who they are. Interact with them accordingly. If your conscience allows, ask them about every part of their life, including parts of their life that are affected by their LGBTQ+ identity. If you are unable to hear certain details of their life, communicate it to them in a way that honors both your faith and their own boundaries, values, and identity (see Chapter 15).

Worship God Alone. I speak with too many parents who make attempts at deepening their relationship with their adult child and believe their efforts are a failure if their child does not reciprocate. To these parents, I want to emphasize your ultimate goal in life. It's not solely about cultivating a profound connection with your child (although that would be wonderful), not just about seeking forgiveness for every past mistake (though we hope for reconciliation), and not even solely about influencing them to turn their hearts toward God (although it's our earnest prayer as parents). Our ultimate objective in life is to become more like Jesus. Amid your efforts to mend, establish, or deepen your connection with your adult child, don't lose sight of this primary goal. God wants you to be close to your child, of course, but he wants you to do it in a way that honors your most central identity—as *his child,* honoring him above all else.

Establish Your Measure of Success. While your child's responses and viewpoints may influence your perception of success in your connection with them, they should not entirely define your measure of success. Consistently practice humility in your self-reflection and when talking to your child, while anchoring yourself to your measure of success, both in individual conversations and in your broader connection with your child. For example, "I acknowledge that I am not a perfect parent, and I've unintentionally hurt my child in the past, with the likelihood of making many more mistakes. They may be upset with me, and there could be validity in their grievances, which I will reflect upon. However, my intention in examining my actions is not solely to gain their favor, reconnect with them, or remain a part of their life. While I hope these outcomes will result from my efforts, my primary goal is to reflect, repent if necessary, and strive toward righteousness because God calls me to." *That* is your measure of success as a parent—to strive to live up to *God's* standard, not your child's.

Require Respect. Though your child is an adult now, there will still be some boundaries they should be expected to maintain. Most notably, being respectful. This is a boundary you should have with everyone in your life, not just your children. If someone is mistreating you, it is good and right to erect stricter and stricter boundaries until they are treating you the way that you deserve as God's child. To be clear, I am not advocating for pop psychology self-respect; what I am advocating is for you to look through the lens of God to see everyone—others, your child, even yourself. You are worthy of respect, not because of who you are, but because of who created you. You are not perfect, you have made lots of mistakes as a parent, and sometimes we, as parents, can allow that guilt to dictate the boundaries we hold for our adult children. But this is a distortion perpetuated by worldly sorrow. We are aiming for godly sorrow,[109] where our core identity is unchanged, even when we mess up. When we allow our adult children to disrespect us, we violate (and allow them to violate) a core godly principle—to strive to treat people the way Jesus did.

Exhort Them Toward Reasonability. Though you and your adult child can absolutely disagree on things and still remain connected, connection will be disrupted if you allow unreasonability to reign. The path to unreasonability starts quickly. If you find that you're repeating yourself, using stronger language, raising your voice, getting annoyed as you recognize you're entering into a familiar territory of unhealthy patterns, or if you notice yourself becoming unreasonable, it's time to stop the conversation until both you and your child are emotionally regulated enough to be reasonable and respectful with each other. If this pattern occurs frequently and consistently disrupts your overall connection with your child, it may be appropriate to consider seeking outside help.

Get Help, If Needed. Perpetuating unhealthy patterns can lead to deeper and deeper wounds for both you and your adult child, and can thus create further disconnection. It might be necessary to lessen the time you speak together for a time in order to heal. It may also be necessary to get some outside help. A family therapist or Christian therapist could be helpful; however, it does not necessarily need to be a mental health professional. It ought to be someone you both feel comfortable with and that can be trusted to honor both of your perspectives, helping to expose some of the unhealthy patterns in your relationship with your child. If your child is unwilling to engage in external help with you, that's okay. You can still proactively seek help independently, aiming to acquire fresh perspectives and a rekindled sense of compassion. This will aid in your efforts to better comprehend the messages your child is attempting to convey.

Should I attend my child's same-sex wedding?

If your child is on the precipice of marrying someone of the same sex, chances are that you have already worked through a lot of grief, shame, and fear regarding your child's sexuality and relationship with God. Their upcoming wedding, however, may trigger some of these big emotions that you thought were gone.

Renewed Grief

Tammy lamented about all the hopes and expectations she was mourning over as she prepared for her daughter's same-sex wedding. "I thought I would get to see her dad walk her down the aisle to another man, that I would only be full of joy on her wedding day and not muddled with grief and fear, and that I would prepare her for her wedding night with a husband."

It's common for parents to be reminded of these often-unspoken hopes and dreams as they are preparing for their child's same-sex wedding. If you are feeling triggered by some of this—that's okay! It's to be expected. It doesn't mean that all that tough inner work you did when your child initially came out is gone. It's still there. It still counts. But that grief and fear will never be gone for good. You will need to continually surrender them before God, especially as new triggers bring them back to the fore. The good news is that you know how to move through these big emotions now. You've done it before.

Wise or Unwise Consideration

Just like with many questions that arise from being a disciple of Jesus on this earth, there is not one specific "right" and one specific "wrong" answer to this; rather, there may be wise and unwise answers based on your own conscience before God. As with any culturally nuanced question that we must sift through in order to find a balanced answer full of both love and righteousness, make sure to spend time before the Lord, listen to the Spirit, and seek mature, spiritual advice.

Don't Prove a Point

You don't need to prove a point with your decision. That's not what this decision is about. This is about your conscience before God. When modern, culturally nuanced situations arise that are not specifically outlined in the Bible, I turn to 1 Peter 3 for guidance, which encourages God's people to seek a clear conscience before him.[110] That is where your focus and efforts should concentrate as you seek guidance from God and trusted spiritual advisers on this.

If you find yourself wanting to make a decision because you want to prove a point to your child by withholding your attendance, please *stop*! This is not the way God parents or loves us and therefore not the way he calls us to love and parent our children. He makes decisions based on love and righteousness, never withholding a portion of his love to teach us a lesson, even when he implements boundaries. You will need to come to a decision in your own personal conscience and determine whether or not your attendance at the wedding insinuates tacit endorsement of the sin.

Parallel Situations

In situations that contain a lot of high emotional and cultural controversy, I like to ask parents to think of a parallel situation and walk me through how they might handle that, in an effort to help them uncover what their conscience will allow. For example, if your child got pregnant (or impregnated someone) out of wedlock with no intention of marrying, would you attend the baby shower? Why or why not?

Walking through a parallel situation may help you to determine what your conscience will allow in this one and avoid making a decision in an emotionally dysregulated state. This also allows us to be consistent in our conviction. We should never allow culture or emotion to dictate our conviction by considering one sin worse than another (like homosexuality over premarital sex).

We Are *for* God

Guy Hammond of Strength in Weakness Ministries likes to say, "People remember what we're *against* more readily than what we are *for*."[111] The truth is that we, as Christians, are not against homosexuality. We are *against* Satan, and we are *for* God.

If you allow this reframe to take root in your heart, it makes a big difference! Homosexuality is simply one of many lies that Satan has woven to turn people away from God. We don't need to villainize homosexuality or those that participate in it. In fact, this would violate God's direction to love everyone and treat each person with kindness, dignity, and respect. No matter what your decision is on this, your child ought to understand that you are not *against* them marrying someone of the same sex, you are *for* God's way of marriage.

Surrender to Their God-Given Free Will

We cannot expect our adult children to live by God's standards if they are not professing Christians. I can't imagine how difficult it would be to not share a deep love for and devotion to our Lord with your child. That is a grief that deserves frequent revisiting as you continually seek to surrender your fear in faith.

But we must respect the free will that God has given our children to choose however they would like to live. We cannot hold them to a standard or an identity that they have not subscribed to. Guy Hammond also likes to point out that there is a difference between agreement and acceptance.[112] We can disagree with someone's decision while still accepting their freedom to decide for themselves. We can similarly disagree with our child's decision while still unconditionally accepting them as they are.

How vs. What

The *how* may be more important than the *what* here. That is, because there is not a clear answer on this specific question in the Bible, *how* you go about making and implementing this decision may be more important than *what* you actually decide. Below are some examples of ways you could communicate your decision to your child:

> **Example:** We have thought, prayed, and gotten advice in this, and we cannot, in good conscience, attend your wedding because it violates a fundamental belief that we hold. It is never our intention to hurt you or disrespect you in any way. We cherish our connection with you. Please know that this has nothing to do with you, it has everything to do with us and our convictions. We would really love to figure out with you other ways in which we can be a part of your life and relationship in a way that honors both you and our faith. We love you so much.

> **Example:** We have thought, prayed, and gotten advice in this and, even though we personally do not agree with your decision to marry someone of the same sex, we wholeheartedly accept you and respect your decision to live your life however you'd like to, therefore we will attend your wedding. We want you to be happy. We happen to believe that God will fulfill you and make you full of joy in a way that this cannot; but we are happy that you are happy. We love you so much.

How should I treat my child's same-sex partner?

Some of the choicest words I have heard from Christian clients have been reserved for their feelings toward their child's same-sex partner. It is agonizing to see your child diverge from your plan for them. It is too easy to harden our pain and grief into anger and direct it all at our child's same-sex romantic partner. "She did this to my daughter!" or "He's the one that brainwashed my son into all of this!" are sentiments I've often heard from Christian parents of LGBTQ+ children.

Though our children are undoubtedly affected by the influence of their peers, especially the ones they are romantically involved with, placing the blame and all our angst on the shoulders of their partner is not helpful or righteous, and it does not uphold God's truth. God tells us that our struggle is not against flesh and blood, but against the spiritual forces of evil.[113]

It's true that your child has been intentionally lied to, but not by their same-sex partner. They've been lied to by Satan. Your child is not alone in this duping effort—Satan has lied to you too. To me. To your child's partner. And to every other human in history. Homosexuality is just one of the many lies of false fulfillment that Satan has sown in our world. You may be powerless in many aspects of your child's sexual orientation, but you are not powerless against Satan. You can walk in the power of the Holy Spirit.[114] Most importantly, God is not powerless against Satan; he has already defeated him.[115] Allow this to ease your anxious heart as you reassess your situation through this truth-filled lens.

Above all else, always remember that we, as Christians, do not treat people the way they deserve to be treated. Instead, we strive to see each person as beloved by God and treat them accordingly. Our respect and kindness for our child's same-sex partner does not stem from *their* worth, it stems from *God's*. We treat them lovingly, not because *they* are worthy, *but because God is.*

Being loving still includes boundaries. It is perfectly appropriate to implement boundaries with your child's same-sex partner, for example, "You cannot speak to me or my child like that in my home" or "We would love to have you for dinner, but we cannot allow you to spend the night with our child in our home." But even boundaries ought to be implemented in love.

This is most certainly a process—and a bumpy one! I never expect that parents of LGBTQ+ children will be able to always see their child's same-sex partner through God's loving eyes, but we ought to strive for this perspective continually. It helps to dwell on our own imperfections and shortcomings before God. We ought to always remember that Jesus did not die for us after we committed to righteousness, no! While we were *still sinners* Christ died for us[116]—for you, for me, *and* for your child's same-sex partner.

Should I call my child by their preferred gender pronoun or name?

I have had some heart-wrenching conversations with parents over the years who have been faced with this reality in their relationship with their child. Below are some things to consider as you are making this decision:

Build in Time to Process

Before you can make a sound decision on how to refer to your transgender child, you might need to work through some grief and fear. If this is a new request from your child and you are still reeling from the shock of them coming out, build in some temporal margins to give yourself enough time to move through the grief, fear, and shame that you may be experiencing.

> **Example:** Honey, I know this request is really important to you. I take it very seriously. Because I want to treat this request properly, I need some time to work through what my conviction is on this. Let's follow up in two weeks with my decision. That should give me enough time to think, pray, and get advice on this. You do not need to ask me between now and then if I've

come to a decision. We will meet in two weeks, and I will share with you my decision then.

Invite Advice

The answer to this question, like so many within this overall discussion, boils down to our personal conscience before God. This means that what one Christian family decides on this will not necessarily be what another Christian family decides. It will be important to get advice on this from trusted spiritual counsel. However, remember that advice is just that—*advice*—not incontrovertible truth. Consider the advice you get in the light of any promptings from the Spirit in order to have a clear conscience before God.

Christian or Not?

Another thing to consider as you are making this decision is whether your child is a Christian or not. If your child is a professing Christian, then you have a duty, both as their parent and their sibling in Christ, to exhort them toward obedience. In this case, obedience regarding the gender binary that God created them in. This, of course, ought to be done lovingly and respectfully as you redirect them to the core components of their identity, which exists completely within Christ.

Weighing Their Autonomy

If your child is not a Christian, your decision may also be influenced by whether or not you still hold parental authority over them (i.e., are they under the age of eighteen or still living in your home?). If they are an adult, live outside your home, or you no longer hold parental authority over them, you may choose to acquiesce and call them by their preferred gender pronoun in order to show respect for the free will God has given them to live however they would like to.

I have heard great arguments on both sides of this question. Parents have justified their decision to not call their child by their preferred gender pronoun or name by stating, "Just because my son *feels* like a girl does not mean that he *is* a girl. He is biologically a male, and no amount of surgery, hormones, or cultural identification can change that. Therefore, I will continue to refer to him as a male because I refuse to feed his delusion that he is a girl." There is certainly great merit in that justification.

Other parents have said to me, "Though I don't believe my daughter is a male, I respect her God-given autonomy to choose how to live and how to identify." There is great merit in this justification as well.

Seek a Clear Conscience

Remember, the most important thing parents can do as they wrestle through this question is to maintain a clear conscience before God. Consider some of the same things from the scenarios offered in previous questions as you grapple with your decision. Especially reflect on whether the *how* is more important than the *what* here. Below are some examples of ways you could communicate your decision to your child.

> **Example:** I have thought, prayed, and gotten advice on this. Although I do not believe that you are a biological female because God created you as a male, I have decided that I will refer to you by your chosen pronoun and name because I respect your God-given autonomy to choose how to live and how to identify. Please be patient with me as I adjust to this. I have referred to you as a male your whole life. If I slip up moving forward, it is not because I am intentionally disrespecting you; it is because I am imperfect.

> **Example:** I have thought, prayed, and gotten advice on this and have decided that I will not be able to call you by your preferred gender pronoun or name. Not only does it go against my faith and conscience, but I also believe that you are not old enough to make this decision on your own. I know this will be a

tough answer for you to contend with. We can revisit this topic in six months. Until then, I'd love to better understand your experience with your gender.

Example: I have thought, prayed, and gotten advice on this and, though I wholeheartedly respect the free will that God has given you to live and identify however you'd like to, it violates my conscience to call you by a pronoun or name that represents a gender that God did not create you as. I hope you know that it is never my intention to bring harm or disrespect to you in any way. I am certainly willing to discuss ways in which I can help you feel more comfortable with your gender while not violating my own faith.

Both...And

Keep in mind that this is not necessarily a "both...and" situation in which you must use or not use both the pronouns and the name. I have known parents to tell their children, "I can't in good conscience call you by your preferred gender pronoun, but I can call you by your preferred name," or vice versa. It's important to consider each of these individually before God as you wrestle through this dual request from your child.

How do I handle shared public restrooms?

As you may have realized by now, I'm not in the business of telling you how to raise your child. I will, however, offer you some things to consider as you weigh this difficult question.

If we think about this logically, bathrooms have never been tied to gender identity or any other social construct. They were originally created to separate people based on *biological sex*, due to differing genitalia, in order to provide privacy and protection.[117]

With that truth in mind, let us also generate some compassion for those who feel uncomfortable using public restrooms that correlate with their biological sex. Going to the bathroom in a public place, no matter who you are, is an extremely vulnerable time. That's why many women have perfected the acrobatic feat of hovering over a public toilet while holding out an arm to a stall door with a broken lock, all the while keeping their lungs inflated with just enough air to bellow out, "Occupied!" lest someone infiltrate this sensitive time.

I can't imagine having to navigate this already delicate task in an environment where I felt that I did not belong, fearful of judgmental stares and hurtful words. No matter what your decision is on this boundary, you can certainly seek to understand and affirm any discomfort your child has with this sensitive situation.

Your decision on this may include many variables, including safety or your child's age and maturity level. A twelve-year-old child who just came out requesting this is very different from a seventeen-year-old who has been identifying as the opposite gender for some time.

No matter what your decision is on this, you will want to refrain from quick, emotionally triggered responses like, "Absolutely not! Are you out of your mind? That's dangerous! I better not ever see you use that bathroom!"

Instead, seek to understand your child's experience as you draw out their underlying desire for using the other bathroom.

> **Example:** Wow, that's a big request. I'll need some time to think, pray, and get advice on it. In the meantime, can you help me understand what using the other bathroom will offer you?

You want to be careful never to shame your child for a request but rather thank them for trusting you and sharing their desire with you. If you decide you will not allow your child to use the opposite bathroom, be sure to communicate it in a loving way, honoring the underlying desire, while setting a boundary on the way that your child brings that desire to fruition. Offer them other ways that you can help them feel comfortable using public restrooms while still staying within the boundaries that you have set for them in their gender expression.

> **Example:** I know this is really important to you, but I cannot allow you to use the bathroom of the opposite sex. That could be dangerous, and it goes against what God wants for us by blurring the boundary lines of gender. But I really want to find a way for you to be comfortable going to the restroom when we are out in public. I can't imagine how uncomfortable it would be to use a bathroom that you don't feel that you belong in. How about you use a single stall or family bathroom instead? This way, you don't have to use a bathroom you don't feel comfortable in, and you remain within the boundary that I've set for you here.

Should I let my daughter wear a binder?

Puberty is a difficult time for most people, but especially for girls as their bodies are morphing into those of women. This awkward and distressing transformation can cause any young woman to want to cover up her body in shame and discomfort. This is only further exacerbated when a young woman identifies as transgender or is uncomfortable in her femininity.

Chest binders are anything used to flatten breast tissue to minimize the breasts' outward appearance. Though there are binders that can be specifically purchased for this, some women resort to other means to achieve the same purpose, like ace bandages, wearing several sports bras at once, or even duct tape.

If your daughter is asking to use a binder, thank her for trusting you with this delicate request. Be careful not to shame her. I know this may evoke a lot of fear for you, but the teenage brain is hyper-rational.[118] The request may be as simple as, "I feel uncomfortable with my breasts, and I heard of a way to minimize my discomfort by using a binder." Be sure to really seek to understand her desire in her request and validate any primary emotions it comes from.

> **Example:** You want to wear a chest binder. I don't know much about chest binders. Can you help me to understand what wearing one would offer you?

> ...I see. You want to wear a binder because you're ashamed of your breasts and you feel like you more closely relate with a male identity.

> That would be really tough to feel so uncomfortable all day, every day with your body. I am so sorry you are experiencing that. Thank you so much for trusting me enough to let me know what you're going through.

As you are making your decision on this, I would highly encourage you to consider the potential physical detriments of wearing a binder. Breast binders can break down breast tissue and even constrict lung function, making it hard to breathe. Our first job as parents is to love our children. We know from God's definition of love in 1 Corinthians 13 that love always protects.[119] Although it is worthwhile to carefully think through every boundary that we implement for our children and allow age-appropriate autonomy within each boundary, this particular request could carry ongoing health risks.

Make sure to communicate your decision to your daughter in a loving and compassionate way, acknowledging and validating her underlying desire to feel comfortable in her body. Work with her to determine ways in which you can allow her to mitigate her discomfort with her body that do not violate the boundaries you have set for her in this.

> **Example:** Honey, though I have a lot of compassion for the discomfort you're feeling with your body right

now, I cannot allow you to wear something that could cause you harm. Let's talk about ways that we can work through your discomfort that won't bring you any harm.

Many parents I've spoken to have offered some of the following options for their daughters as they are navigating discomfort with their bodies: discussing and normalizing the discomfort with their daughter, having their daughter join a teen support group to discuss common discomfort in the body, sharing personal experiences from when the parent went through puberty, wearing certain items of clothing (e.g., a sweatshirt) to mitigate the exposure of breasts, wearing a single sports bra to mitigate the exposure of breasts, etc. There are lots of options you could offer to your daughter that do not compromise her safety.

Should I allow my child to dress in opposite-sex clothing?

As with other questions of this nature, the answer will depend on a variety of factors, most notably your personal conscience before God and whether your child is still held to your set of values at this point in their development. Before you decide, seek to understand your child's experience, and validate what you can.

> **Example:** It makes a lot of sense that you want to be comfortable in the clothing you wear. I want that for you too!

Set a timeline for your child in which you will make this decision. Be sure to give yourself enough time to move through your big emotions, pray, get advice, and contemplate your conscience before God. Once you've made your decision, be sure to communicate it to your child in a loving and transparent way that acknowledges any difficulty they may have with it. If there are additional boundaries around the decision you've made, be sure to communicate them clearly.

Example: Son/Daughter, it breaks my heart that you have been feeling so uncomfortable in your body and in your clothes recently. I really want to find a way that you can feel more comfortable that is also congruent with our family values and God's statutes. Though I cannot allow you to shop in the women's/men's department, I can take you to another store that might have clothes you like better.

Example: I am willing to let you shop in the women's/men's department. However, I will need to approve the item or outfit before it is purchased and worn to ensure it is not too feminine/masculine.

Should I let my child undergo hormone therapy?

No human can tell you how to raise your own child, least of all me. Every parent will have to come to a decision on this as they weigh what's best for their child, their own conscience before God, and the boundaries and values that exist in their home. That said, I often get asked which hill I would personally be willing to die on with my own children—and this is it.

As you are weighing different factors in this decision, consider the potential health risks and long-term consequences for anyone receiving cross-sex hormone therapy (CHT). Long-term use causes irreversible changes to both primary and secondary sex characteristics, including tone of voice, facial hair, breast tissue, etc. Long-term use has also been linked to infertility.[120]

These effects can be devastating for anyone, but especially those who later choose to detransition and return back to their natal sex. In any other circumstance, that hormonal level would be considered pathological.[121] CHT essentially *infects* natal females with a pathological amount of testosterone (the diagnosis is polycystic ovary syndrome, or PCOS) and men with a pathological amount of estrogen (the diagnosis is hypogonadism) in order to achieve their desired gender expression.

If your child has not yet gone through puberty, you may have heard a justification for puberty blockers to allow your child time to contemplate their desired gender expression. "It's a pause button as you consider your options," many gender-affirming pediatricians and endocrinologists may say. Lupron (once used to chemically castrate sex offenders) is the go-to drug for pausing puberty.

The very least I could say about this is that there have been an alarmingly low number of studies done on the effects of intentionally intervening in puberty in this way. Perhaps that is why the FDA does not approve of this practice. What's more, not only does pausing puberty put your child behind their peers in terms of physical development, but it could potentially affect their brain development as well. Hormones are coursing through the preteen and teenage brains during puberty, and we simply do not yet know the effects on the brain if puberty is blocked.[122]

Remember that your priority to love your child and protect them outweighs your desire to want to be friends with or liked by your child. It also outweighs any desire to avoid stirring up disagreement in your home. I know many parents who are not comfortable with their child's request on this or another potentially harmful request, but they acquiesce because they are afraid of their child's reaction if they were to say no. This is not the way of God! God does not parent us based on our potential reactions. He parents us based on what's best for us. If you find yourself often going against your conscience in order to mitigate your child's response, you may have a power imbalance in your home. You, the parent, ought to hold more power than your child.

To be clear, I am not suggesting that you wield your power in a destructive or overbearing way. But just as God holds more power than us in our relationship with him, so the power you hold over your child ought to assure them that they are *safe* with you. They can trust you to make decisions for them while they are not yet able to do so fully for themselves. Is this not the surrender and trust we are asked to have with our heavenly Parent, God? If you are frequently making decisions in order to keep the peace in the home, assess the power dynamic within your family. You may need to redistribute some of the power so that you are making decisions rooted in love and protection, not fear.

How do I deal with rapid-onset gender dysphoria?

If you are the parent or loved one of someone experiencing ROGD, the sudden and intense identification of a different gender among adolescents, chances are that you are reeling in shock along with the typical grief, shame, fear, and hurt that most Christian parents experience when their child comes out. You are not alone. This is the number one growing phenomenon among teenage girls. One study showed a 2000 percent increase in just seven years.[123] This phenomenon has become a social epidemic. We saw this same thing happen fifty years ago with anorexia. It's not that this phenomenon isn't a legitimate experience for some, but because there are significant social components, it has created a social contagion.

Resources

There is so much to say about ROGD that it could take up a whole separate book. Fortunately, Abigail Shrier has already written that book in *Irreversible Damage: The Transgender Craze Seducing Our Daughters*. She provides a thorough overview of ROGD and explanations about the growing epidemic, and offers some potential avenues to help those in our lives struggling with ROGD. Though Shrier does not write from a Christian perspective, she offers some important perspectives that Christians dealing with this in their homes ought to consider. Preston Sprinkle's *Embodied* also gives a great understanding of ROGD. I have compiled other notable resources for parents of ROGD children on my website, www.heartsetabove.com.

ROGD → Identity

Every human suffers from an identity issue. We are all desperate to know who we are, what makes up our worth, and if we are loved and valued. This identity investigation starts from the very beginning of our lives and continues to the end of it, but there is a huge peak in adolescence.

Remember how awful it was to be a preteen, teenager, and young adult? Spiraling in a seemingly endless pursuit of identity and worth, exacerbated by a flood of hormones throwing off your equilibrium, while lacking a fully functioning brain to boot! You could not pay me enough to go back to that time in my life when insecurity and fear reigned.

We currently live in a culture that elevates the oppressed (not a political statement, simply a cultural observation). Identifying with a marginalized group can offer a quick boost in social status among our youth. Imagine how enticing and easy it would be as a teenager in the current cultural climate to simply identify as a member of the LGBTQ+ community. There is no major pushback on a cultural level, there is no burden of proof placed on the identifier, and there is an automatic bump in social status. Why wouldn't young people want to jump on this bandwagon?

I am not at all suggesting that teenagers experiencing ROGD are lying about their gender dysphoria. I am suggesting that we live in a culture that too quickly points people to gender dysphoria if they are experiencing even slight discomfort with their body, with stereotypical gender norms, or with insecurities in identity. But who doesn't struggle with either their body, gender norms, or their identity, *especially* in adolescence?

If we reframe ROGD as an identity issue and not a biological issue, we are dealing with something every human can relate to. Fortunately, we were created by a God who values us beyond our comprehension. We are so worthy to him that he died for us! That's way more significant than a "like" on social media!

In fact, God is so enamored with your child (and you!) that he gave them multiple identity markers to try to even begin to express his deep fondness for them. If it's an identity our children are so desperate for, let's give them some identity! Let's show them who they are before God, who they were created to be. I guarantee it fulfills the heart way more than any identity label the world can offer. Below are just a few identities God is eager to give each of us:

Never alone Deuteronomy 31:8

Wonderfully made Psalm 139:14

Washed clean Isaiah 1:18
Secure Jeremiah 29:11
Beloved Jeremiah 31:3
Delighted in Zephaniah 3:17
Adopted into God's family Romans 8:15
Coheir with Christ Romans 8:17
A coworker 1 Corinthians 3:9
New 2 Corinthians 5:17
An ambassador for Christ 2 Corinthians 5:20
Righteous 2 Corinthians 5:21
A temple of the Holy Spirit 1 Corinthians 6:19
A pleasing aroma 2 Corinthians 2:15
Bold 2 Corinthians 3:12
Free Galatians 5:1
A masterpiece Ephesians 2:10 NLT
Whole Colossians 2:10
Set apart 1 Peter 2:9
A child of God 1 John 2:1

If your child is struggling through ROGD, seek to understand their experience while reminding them of the identity they have in God and in your family. Maintain ongoing connection with them to help them develop a holistic understanding of their complete identity, instead of spotlighting their gender identity as the most significant part of self. Consider limiting their exposure to a constant barrage of trans advocacy. Help them to get involved with many different kinds of friend groups, influences, and activities to aid in their development of a healthy identity diet (see Chapter 4).

How do I respond to, "I have to be true to myself"?

So often pop psychology contains a form of godliness but denies its true power (as a mental health professional, I'm allowed to say that, right?) How often have we heard psychologists, celebrities, influencers, friends, and family members excuse their sin by saying something like, "I have to be unapologetically me." As Christians, we are often tempted to roll our eyes at this modern, earthly sentiment, but actually, *I wholeheartedly agree!* We DO have to be true to ourselves, unapologetically and fully who we are! *I just don't see how we can do that outside of God.*

Being true to myself *IS* being wrapped up in Christ. Living my truth *IS* obeying out of my love for God. Being unapologetically me *IS* striving to become the person that God intended for me to be. Only as I get closer to God can I become my "true self." Who knows my true self better than my Creator, who carefully knit me together in my mother's womb[124] and knows every hair on my head?[125] Without God at the center of this sentiment, it makes no sense. Put God at the center of your life and you will continually become your true self, *hidden with Christ in God.*[126]

How do I handle my Christian child's pro-gay theology stance?

I had a memorable conversation with Brenda once about her adult Christian daughter, Carla, who had recently entered into a same-sex relationship. Carla had not walked away from God completely; she claimed that he was still central to her life. But she had recently engaged with some pro-gay theology and concluded that entering into a same-sex romantic relationship was permitted by God as long as it was monogamous and no premarital sexual activity occurred.

After Brenda acknowledged and talked through her grief and fear a bit, I said to her, "The good news is that, though you and Carla have a theological difference on a matter you consider to be a primary issue, you have more in common with her than not. You both still share the most fundamental aspect of your faith—you both love God and desire to live for him."

Brenda was moved to tears over my affirmation of the love her daughter had for God, even in the midst of her new pro-gay conviction. "So, you think she's still saved?" she asked me.

Well, that's an entirely different matter that no human can ever answer. God gives us lots of information, insight, and power as humans on earth, but he never allows for us to speak to the eternal status of another before him. We can trust that, if someone loves God and is actively seeking out the truth, God will seek to honor them as they honor him. We know that God is not in the business of hiding the truth from those who pursue it.[127]

But the path to truth is often muddled with emotion, fleshly desire, wrong turns, and cultural influence. There is room for us as parents to disagree with our children's theological conclusions, even if it is surrounding an issue that we consider to be fundamental. I am *not* saying you ought to acquiesce to their newfound theological conviction. I *am* suggesting that, just as I (a Protestant Christian) navigate relationships with my Catholic friends and family members, you can absolutely affirm your child's *love for and devotion to God*, even if you have theological disagreements. Meanwhile, always trust that the Spirit will prompt you to exhort toward the truth if and when the time presents itself.

What if I'm doing all that I can?

Sometimes you're doing all you can, but that doesn't necessarily mean you will have your desired result. Your measure of success cannot be your child's behavioral compliance. Your measure of success must aim higher than that: striving to love your child with the love of the Lord.

Look how people responded when Jesus showed his love for them. Some of them crumbled before him, desperate to seek more of what he offered. And some of them hardened before him, running from the very thing they wanted so desperately but didn't recognize was standing right in front of them. Our kids' response to our love cannot be our measure of success.

When you are doing all you can with your child, your job is to be like the prodigal son's father. He didn't chase after his son, guilting him into compliance with smothering affirmations or manipulating him into obedience by withholding his love and affection. He did all he could, then he waited. And he *waited well.*

What if my child is not in heaven with me?

Although no parent has ever asked me this question with these exact words, this is usually the terrified sentiment underlying many a fear-induced question. To be sure, this is one of our most agonizing anxieties as Christian parents. This is the kind of concern that keeps us up late at night, tossing and turning in despair. It is our greatest foundational hope that our children will know and love God, such that they will be with him for eternity. This hope undergirds and permeates everything we do as Christian parents. Let's remember a few key things as we preserve this hope in faith, not fear.

It's Not Clear

God does not make it abundantly clear to us who exactly will be in heaven and who will not be. Instead of inserting ourselves outside our purview, let's instead focus on what God has made apparent to us. He makes it clear that we are to love him first and with everything we've got. He makes it clear that we are to love others before ourselves and unconditionally. He makes it clear how tenderly and deeply he loves us, his children, by the love he allows us to have for our own children. These are the things he is most definitive in. Let God have what is his to control—the eternal status of all. You focus on what he has put within your control—loving him and others. Surrender the rest.

It's You and God First

My incredibly wise mentor, colleague, sister in Christ, and friend, Dr. Jennifer Konzen—a marriage and family therapist, certified sex therapist, world-renowned researcher, and educator—was recently asked this question about her relationship with her own children. She shared the anguish this has often brought her and confirmed that, given the chance, she would happily surrender her own salvation so that her children could be saved instead. Then she said something that moved me to tears because it was simultaneously beautiful and heartbreaking, "I had to get to a place where I just surrendered to the fact that, at the end of the day, it's just me and God. It just has to be."[128]

Is this not what Luke 14:26 refers to when Jesus tells us that we must love him so far beyond how we love anyone else? When we counted the cost of following Christ, part of our deliberation was that even if our mother, our father, yes, even our very children, chose a different path, we would remain on the narrow path that leads to God. There is something gloriously noble, loyal, and beautiful about unwaveringly holding to our covenant vow before the Lord in this way. But it doesn't take away the agony of it. Run to God in your fear and your grief. No one understands better than he, for he mourns over all his children that will not be with him for eternity.

It's About the Relationship

Don't let the promise of heaven eclipse our true hope for our children—*to know and love God*. It's true that heaven is a promise given to God's people, but heaven is not the *reason* that we live for God. In fact, if I were to ask a fellow sibling in the faith, "Why do you deny yourself daily, making yourself obedient to the Lord?" and they responded with, "Because I want to go to heaven," I would be pretty concerned.

God calls us to obey out of our love for him,[129] not out of our desire for a cushy eternity. Let us never forget why we live for God—*because he died for us*. We love because he first loved us,[130] enough to give up his life. This is why we do what we do as Christians. We don't want to give our kids the wrong idea by warping our motivation with the promise of heaven.

When we make heaven our sole motivation for living for Christ, we lose the fundamental relational aspect and quickly turn pharisaical, focusing on behavior modification instead of the heart. This is the opposite of how God calls us to live and the opposite of what he calls us to instill in the hearts of our children. Let's properly set the frame of our own hearts so that we do not mislead our kids in this. Our biggest hope is that our children will have a deep, intimate, and rich *relationship* with God.

Author's Note

People are often curious about what it's like to serve God in this field. Things that you only talk to your spouse, your best friend, your pastor, or your therapist about—for example, your sex life, shame from childhood, and core insecurities of unworthiness—I talk about to public audiences. It is...a lot of things!

Exhausting

Though I am a serious introvert, and this type of work can deplete my energy, as it requires me to spend most of my time talking with people, it is exhausting in a whole different way as well. The messy middle space, where Jesus often stood, is not a popular place to be. It's much easier to take a stance on the extremes of an issue. If you exist in an extreme, you at least have lots of support from one side that helps to bolster your morale when the other side vehemently objects.

When you exist in the messy middle, there is disagreement from *both sides*. People on the more liberal side of this issue have said to me, "How dare you even suggest that homosexuality/crossing gender boundaries is sinful!" And people on the more conservative side of this issue, equally enraged, have exclaimed, "How dare you befriend, interact with, and show love or respect toward gay and trans people!"

When you exist in the messy middle, people on both extremes are constantly ready to attack. Not only do I need to continue to grow internally in this area, but I also have to do it on the defense, which is exhausting.

Unrelenting

I've never had a burning bush[131] moment where, barefoot and trembling, I heard God plainly say to me, "ELLEN, YOU MUST SERVE ME IN THIS WAY!" So I am not completely comfortable using the word "calling" to describe this work that I do for the Lord. However, I do feel an unrelenting compulsion to this type of service. Sometimes I am passionate and excited about this compulsion, overcome with gratitude that I get to serve in this way. And sometimes I beg God to take the compulsion away. Truly, my life would be so much easier if I did not feel compelled to serve in this way.

Not only would I be spared from publicly sharing some of the most intimate details of my life, but I also would be able to focus more on my day job. Unfortunately, the messy middle space is also the space that is devoid of funding. Few people want to support a ministry that is in such a controversial area and especially one that seeks to exist in the messy middle. The organizations on the extremes of this issue receive a lot of funding, to be sure! But not those of us in the messy middle.

I have often wrestled with confusion before God, wondering why he would put this unrelenting compulsion on my heart if it didn't at least provide a living. I have prayed many times for a way to make this act of service my day job, but God has not provided this for me as of yet. Instead, I maintain a small therapy practice to pay the bills, so that I can continue to serve in this way.

I have to constantly fight for balance in my focus. Though I want to spend *all* my work time on matters of sex, sexuality, and gender, I often have to pull my focus from that in order to properly attend to my therapy practice. I am confident that God has a purpose in this particular path of mine, but it can sometimes feel confusing and jarring.

Faith-Building

When I first became a Christian, I begged God that he would use me as he sees fit, that I would be his vessel, his hands and feet to do with as he willed. My heart swells with gratitude that God answered this prayer so unmistakably.

In those moments when I slip into ingratitude and faithlessness, I reminisce on this early prayer of mine and stand in awe of God's answer. This unrelenting compulsion reminds me daily of the devotion I continually offer to the Lord by awakening the sentiment expressed in Galatians 2:20, "I have been crucified with Christ and I no longer live, but Christ lives in me. The life I now live in the body, I live by faith in the Son of God, who loved me and gave himself for me."

Demanding

LGBTQ+ discussions are some of the most highly contested and controversial topics in our world today, not to mention our churches. Because many parents have elevated this in their hearts as one of their greatest fears, they often do not want to preemptively educate themselves on these topics. Instead, they hope and pray that they will be spared this anticipated devastation.

When the dreaded fear becomes a reality for some people, manners tend to go out the window as they enter full-blown crisis mode. What can escalate this already tense time is when parents want a succinct, action-based answer from me to quickly remedy the "problem." Unfortunately, such an answer does not exist.

The direction I give to parents usually starts on a heart level and requires systemic repentance and perspective shifts on their part. Though this kind of change is quite effective, it is not quick, easy, or fun. This can further fuel parents' panic. Two a.m. phone calls, insistent emails like, "My son just came out; you *need* to call me now!!" and angry outbursts like, "Shut up! I don't care about all of that! Just tell me exactly what I should say to my daughter to get her to stop!" become part of my reality when parents enter into this state of crisis.

While I have copious amounts of empathy and compassion for parents experiencing this and completely understand how rationale and courtesy can go out the window while in panic, truth be told, this can really wear on me. I have to continually fight for a godly perspective.

Before I speak with anyone about LGBTQ+ topics, I always beg God to allow me to see the other person (or people) through his eyes. This has often helped me not take it personally when these panic-induced demands come my way but instead to see that person for what they really are—a terrified child of God.

Incredibly Rewarding and Inspiring

For every demanding, panicky parent, there are ten abundantly grateful and gracious parents that I encounter. It is so moving to watch people bravely walk into the fire and be willingly refined for the sake of both their love for God and their love for their child. To get to witness that kind of valiant obedience, courageous surrender, and tenacious faith day in and day out inspires me greatly and spurs me on in my own faith.

Hilariously Humbling

You know the kind of humility that comes from God giving you what you always wanted, but not in the way you expected it? I get to experience that a lot. Like many kids growing up, I dreamed of one day having some kind of notoriety. I naturally assumed this would come in the form of international stardom. In fact, in grade school, I practiced my "famous signature" several times in preparation for my combination acting/singing career (the small obstacle of not being able to sing or act did not occur to me at the time). Instead, God gave me a different kind of notoriety—the kind that *doesn't* make your head swell.

I attended a women's retreat several years ago. I was drying my hands in the restroom when someone walked in and saw me, did a double take, and exclaimed, "I know you! Aren't you the…the…"

Clearly realizing she didn't know how to finish the sentence politely, her words trailed off while she just stood there helplessly looking to me for rescue. After embracing the awkward for a few seconds, I finally decided to extricate her from her social agony and said, "The former lesbian? Yep, that's me!"

I had a good laugh with God as I realized that he did in fact allow me notoriety, just not in the way my eight-year-old self anticipated. Instead, he gave me the opportunity to boast in my weaknesses for his glory, while desperately having to rely on him to do so. I definitely wouldn't trade this reality for what my eight-year-old self had in mind!

"How Does That Work?"

People also are very curious about how I can be happily married to a man that I bore two children with, while simultaneously being attracted to women. "How does that work?" people usually ask (say hello to the title of my next book). Well, I would love to tell you! But it would take a whole other book to do so. One that I hope to write just as soon as I take a long vacation to recuperate from writing this book.

Acknowledgments

I could not serve God and his people in this capacity or have written this book without an entire village of support around me.

Of course, without God's unconditional, unfathomable, perfect love and parenting, I could not have contextualized any of the concepts in this book.

To my husband, who models so much of God's love and character—I could never have mustered the safety and courage it takes to serve God in this capacity (including writing this book) without you. In the cacophony of a world that has strayed so far from Eden, you model God's steadfast fortress of safety in my life, and I love retreating in God with you. You also willingly let me take hours away from you and our family to talk about every intimate detail of our life—the good, the bad, and the ugly. What a testament to your courage, sacrifice, and devotion to our God. Though I know it's my voice people hear and my words people read, you are intertwined in so much of what I say and do. Also, big thanks to you and the kids for putting up with things like muffins and mac and cheese for dinner on COVID-filled nights of writing.

To my parents, who exuded imperfect, yet pretty darn good parenting, I am so grateful for your continued love, support, and guidance in everything I do. I deeply admire your willingness to look your imperfections in the eye, unashamed, while simultaneously standing firm and secure in God's perfection. So much of how I see the world is due to the way you taught me to strive to see things from God's perspective. 2 Samuel 7:18, "Who am I, Sovereign LORD, and what is my family, that you have brought me this far?" has always been our desperately grateful cry to God as a family. I feel that more and more every day and am in awe of how you have stewarded our family toward that frame of heart. My gratitude for you and admiration toward you is beyond what words can express.

To my in-laws, who provide countless hours of babysitting, laundry folding, dinners, and listening ears, you have been the true hands and feet of Jesus to me and my family. Your love and support have often salved my weary heart, mind, body, and soul. Your incredible example of servitude and generosity is humbling and convicting, and I strive to imitate it in the way that I serve God and his people. I am so grateful to be one of the many recipients of your love and sacrifice.

To Guy and Laura Hammond and the entire Strength in Weakness Ministry staff, I am continually moved and inspired by your heart to serve God in this incredibly tender and vulnerable way. This is often a lonely battlefield to be on, and I am proud and honored to stand on it side by side with each of you. There is no way I could have maintained the heart to serve in this way for so long without your example of constant, immovable, and steadfast faith and devotion. You have spurred me on continually through the years, and this book is a direct reflection of that.

To the parents who allow me to serve them in this capacity, I am continually moved by your perseverance, faith, surrender, and immovable devotion to our God and to your children. You inspire me daily.

It is a special relationship that an author has with her editor(s). It requires a lot of vulnerability to expose one's raw, unpolished thoughts to another, especially on such a controversial topic. I am so grateful to Christy, Renee, Shauna, Elizabeth, Gina, and Amy for treating this vulnerable act with such consideration, tenderness, and excellence.

To the entire Morgan James team, I extend my heartfelt gratitude. Your fearless decision to embrace this contentious book amid our culturally turbulent times is truly motivating. In this arid cultural landscape, your courage and support have been a welcome refuge, offering invaluable encouragement to me.

And finally, to my husband's sweatpants and hoodies, I could not have possibly written this book without the hours of comfort you have provided me while I have toiled over word choice, agonized over content placement, and fought for the most potent and efficient way to express these ideas.

About the Author

Ellen is a faithful Christian woman, wife, and mother. She is also same-sex attracted. While growing up in a Christian home, Ellen and her family had to navigate the nuances of her sexual orientation. Ellen is married to the love of her life, her husband, and together they also must navigate the unique realities of her sexual orientation and her past as a lesbian.

Ellen has a BA in interpersonal communication from East Carolina University and an MA in counseling from Harding School of Theology. She is a licensed marriage and family therapist (LMFT) and a licensed clinical mental health counselor (LCMHC). Since 2010 Ellen has walked alongside individuals as they navigate the joys and difficulties of striving for sexual integrity as outlined by the historically Christian perspective of the biblical sexual ethic.

Both in her service as chief operating officer with Strength in Weakness Ministries and through her consultation business, Heart Set Above, Ellen has helped countless individuals and families navigate the tender topics of sexual identity and gender identity while remaining rooted in their faith.

Endnotes

1   B. M. Newman and P. R. Newman, *Development Through Life: A Psychosocial Approach* (Stamford, CT: Cengage Learning, 2015).

2   Exodus 20:11.

3   Newman and Newman, 272.

4   Newman and Newman, 272.

5   Newman and Newman, 272.

6   Newman and Newman, 272.

7   Newman and Newman, 272.

8   This is certainly not the only way that distortions around sexual and gender identity can form, but one of them.

9   Manning, B., Blasé, J., & Foreman, J. (2015). *ABBA's Child: The Cry of the Heart for Intimate Belonging.* NavPress; Schwartz, R. C., & Sweezy, M. (2020). *Internal Family Systems Therapy.* The Guilford Press; LaCroix, M. (2021). *Restoring Relationship: Transforming Fear Into Love Through Connection.* Mollylacroix.com.

10 B. M. Newman and P. R. Newman, *Lifespan Development* (Stamford, CT: Cengage Learning, 2003), 315.

11 Matthew 25:14–30.

12 D.J. Siegal, *Brainstorm: The Power and Purpose of the Teenage Brain* (New York: TarcherPerigee, 2014), 75–76.

13 Siegel, *Brainstorm*, 75–76.

14 Siegel, 18–22.

15 Siegel, 18–22.

16 Siegel, 18–22.

17   Siegel, 18–22.

18   Newman and Newman, *Development Through Life*, 272.

19   Genesis 16:13, HCSB.

20   Romans 3:23.

21   Matthew 5:48; Philippians 3:12.

22   Hebrews 4:16.

23   2 Corinthians 12:9.

24   Luke 2:19.

25   John 14:15.

26   Preston M. Sprinkle (Host). 2017, December 4). Wealth or Poverty?—Divorce and Same-Sex Marriage—Conquest in Exodus? (No. 623) [Audio podcast episode]. In Theology in the Raw, https://theologyintheraw.com/podcast/623-wealth-or-poverty-divorce-and-same-sex-marriage-conquest-in-exodus/.

27   Tim and Dr. Jennifer Konzen, *Redeemed Sexuality: A Guide to Sexuality for Christian Singles, Campus Students, Teens and Parents* (Nashville, TN: Elm Hill, 2018), 8–9.

28   E. Perel (n.d.), Focus on Eroticism, retrieved June 15, 2022, from https://www.estherperel.com/focus-on-categories/eroticism.

29   Preston M. Sprinkle, *A Biblical Theology of Marriage,* Digital Leaders Forum (2018), https://www.digitalleadersforum.org/courses/take/digital-leaders-forum.

30   A comprehensive sexual education should also encompass a biblical perspective on celibacy. For guidance on restoring God's intended purpose for celibacy, see Chapter 9.

31   Douglas E. Rosenau, *A Celebration of Sex* (Nashville, TN: Thomas Nelson, 2002), 2–5.

32   Rosenau, *A Celebration of Sex*, 2–5.

33   1 Corinthians 9:22.

34   Ephesians 4:26.

35   Guy Hammond, *Caring Beyond the Margins: What Every Christian Needs to Know About Homosexuality* (Spring, TX: Illumination Publishers, 2012).

36   Living Out. (2021). "Marriage as a Trailer." Articles | Living Out. Retrieved November 7, 2023, from https://www.livingout.org/resources/articles/69/

marriage-as-a-trailer.

37 Rosenau, *A Celebration of Sex*, 2–5.

38 1 Corinthians 7:9.

39 Genesis 1:27.

40 Preston M. Sprinkle, *Introduction to the Transgender Conversation*, Digital Leaders Forum (2018), https://www.digitalleadersforum.org/courses/take/digital-leaders-forum.

41 Sprinkle, *Introduction to the Transgender Conversation*.

42 Preston M. Sprinkle, *Embodied* (Colorado Springs, CO: David C. Cook 2021), 71.

43 Sprinkle, *Embodied*, 71.

44 Genesis 2:18, 20.

45 Sprinkle, *Introduction to the Transgender Conversation*.

46 Sprinkle, *Introduction to the Transgender Conversation*.

47 Sprinkle, *Introduction to the Transgender Conversation*.

48 Genesis 2:18, 24.

49 Christopher West, *Our Bodies Tell God's Story: Discovering the Divine Plan for Love, Sex, and Gender* (Ada, MI: Brazos Press, 2020), 39.

50 Sprinkle, *Introduction to the Transgender Conversation*.

51 J. Harris, R. Monje, G. Marutsky, V. Koha, B. Perkins, S. G. Kinnard, G. Giles, S. Lewis, J. Shaw, S. Warlow, and K. S. McKean, *The Bible and Gender: Roles, Leadership, and Ministry* (Spring, TX: Illumination Publishers, 2020), 10.

52 Exodus 25–27; 2 Samuel 6; 1 Chronicles 22, 28.

53 Matthew 28:1–7; Mark 16:1–13; Luke 24; John 20; Acts 1:1–10.

54 Sprinkle, *Embodied*, 69–70.

55 Psalm 139:14.

56 Lisa Littman, "Parent Reports of Adolescents and Young Adults Perceived to Show Signs of a Rapid Onset of Gender Dysphoria," *PLOS ONE* 13, no. 8 (2018), 10–33, https://doi.org/10.1371/journal.pone.0202330.

57 Mark A. Yarhouse, *Understanding Gender Dysphoria: Navigating Transgender Issues in a Changing Culture* (Chicago, IL: IVP Academic, 2015), 17.

58 Isaiah 46:3; Isaiah 49:14–15; Isaiah 66:13.

59 John 11:35.

60 Matthew 26:38; Hebrews 5:7.

61 Matthew 23:37.

62 John 13:8–9.

63 Luke 10:25–37.

64 1 Samuel 16:11.

65 2 Samuel 6:14–22.

66 1 Samuel 20:41.

67 Judges 4.

68 Judges 4.

69 Ruth 2–3.

70 1 Samuel 25.

71 Proverbs 31.

72 Sprinkle, *Embodied*, 83.

73 Luke 15:1.

74 Psalm 34:18.

75 Matthew 5:4.

76 Exodus 17:11.

77 Hebrews 10:25.

78 Revelation 3:20.

79 R. B. Ardito and D. Rabellino, "Therapeutic alliance and outcome of psychotherapy: Historical excursus, measurements, and prospects for research," *Frontiers in Psychology*, 18 October 2011, 9, https://www.ncbi.nlm.nih.gov/pmc/articles/PMC3198542/.

80 "LGBTQI," NAMI, accessed February 9, 2023. https://www.nami.org/Your-Journey/Identity-and-Cultural-Dimensions/LGBTQI.

81 S. T. Russell, and K. Joyner, "Adolescent sexual orientation and suicide risk: Evidence from a national study," *American Journal of Public Health* (August 2001), https://www.ncbi.nlm.nih.gov/pmc/articles/PMC1446760/, 1276.

82 Science and Nonduality (2021). The Wisdom of Trauma. Retrieved October 10, 2023, from https://thewisdomoftrauma.com/?utm_source=ActiveCampaign&utm_medium=email&utm_content=%F0%9F%A7%A1+Watch+The+Wisdom+of+Trauma+and+Continue+Learning&utm_campaign=TheWisdomofTrauma+com+New+Website+Announcement+2nd+Email.

83 Hebrews 13:8.

84 Luke 22:61.

85 Abigail Shrier, *Irreversible Damage: The Transgender Craze Seducing Our Daughters* (Washington, D.C.: Regnery, 2020),59–78.

86 M. K. Laidlaw, Q. L. Van Meter, P. W. Hruz, A. Van Mol, and W. J. Malone, "Endocrine Treatment of Gender-dysphoric/Gender-incongruent Persons: An Endocrine Society Clinical Practice Guideline" [letter to the editor], *The Journal of Clinical Endocrinology & Metabolism* 104, no. 3 (March 2019), 686, https://doi.org/10.1210/jc.2018-01925.

87 John 15:15.

88 1 Samuel 18.

89 Exodus 20:3.

90 Isaiah 55:8–9.

91 M. L. Chivers, G. Rieger, E. Latty, and J. M. Bailey, "A Sex Difference in the Specificity of Sexual Arousal," *Psychological Science* 15, no. 11 (2004), 331, doi: 10.1111/j.0956-7976.2004.00750.x, PMID: 15482445.

92 V. M. Durand and D. H. Barlow, *Essentials of Abnormal Psychology* (Stamford, CT: Cengage Learning 2016), 329.

93 Lisa Diamond quoted in Jenna A. Glover, Renee V. Galliher & Trenton G. Lamere (2009) "Identity Development and Exploration Among Sexual Minority Adolescents: Examination of a Multidimensional Model," *Journal of Homosexuality* 56, no. 1, 83, DOI: 10.1080/00918360802551555.

94 Rosenau, *A Celebration of Sex*, 2–5.

95 J. P. Calzo, T. C. Antonucci, V. M. Mays, and S. D. Cochran, "Retrospective recall of sexual orientation identity development among gay, lesbian, and bisexual adults," *Developmental Psychology* 47, no. 6 (2011), 1658–1673, doi:10.1037/a0025508; M. A. Yarhouse, E. S. Tan, and L. M. Pawlowski, "Sexual Identity Development and Synthesis among LGB-identified and LGB Dis-identified Persons," *Journal of Psychology and Theology* 33, no. 1 (2005), 3–16.

96 Calzo, et. al., "Retrospective recall," 1658–1673; Yarhouse, et. al., "Sexual Identity Development," 3–16.

97 Calzo, et. al., 3–16.

98 Sprinkle, *Introduction to the Transgender Conversation*.

99   Lisa Diamond, "Lisa Diamond on Sexual Fluidity of Men and Women," Cornell University, 17 October 2013, https://www.youtube.com/watch?v=m2rTHDOuUBw, 4:32.

100   Diamond, "Lisa Diamond on Sexual Fluidity of Men and Women," 17:09.

101   Preston M. Sprinkle (Host), "Are Puberty Blockers and Cross-Sex Hormones Safe? Dr. Michael Laidlaw," Theology in the Raw [audio podcast], 6 May 2021, https://www.patheos.com/editorial/podcasts/theology-in-the-raw/2021/864--are-puberty-blockers-and-crosssex-hormones-safe-dr-michael-laidlaw.

102   Shrier, *Irreversible Damage*, 161–162.

103   Matthew 19:12.

104   Sprinkle, *Embodied*, 95–111.

105   Sprinkle, *Embodied*, 95–111.

106   National Institute of Mental Health. (2020). LGBTQ+. U.S. Department of Health and Human Services, National Institute of Health. Retrieved August 11, 2023, from https://www.nami.org/Your-Journey/Identity-and-Cultural-Dimensions/LGBTQ#:~:text=LGB%20adults%20are%20more%20than,experience%20a%20mental%20health%20condition.

107   Cecilia Dhejne, et al., "Long-Term Follow-Up of Transsexual Persons Undergoing Sex Reassignment Surgery: Cohort Study in Sweden," PLoS One 6, no. 2 (2011): e16885, https://doi.org/10.1371/journal.pone.0016885.

108   Paul W. Hruz, Lawrence S. Mayer, and Paul R. McHugh, "Growing Pains: Problems with Puberty Suppression in Treating Gender Dysphoria," New Atlantis, Spring 2017, https:// www.thenewatlantis.com/publications/growing-pains ("Whether puberty suppression is safe and effective when used for gender dysphoria remains unclear and unsupported by rigorous scientific evidence").

109   2 Corinthians 7:10.

110   1 Peter 3:16–22.

111   Guy Hammond, *Gay & Christian? How Pro-Gay Theology Is Crashing into the Church Like a Speeding Train without a Whistle* (Illumination Publishers, 2021), 142–43.

112   Hammond, *Gay & Christian?*, 126–27.

113   Ephesians 6:12.

114 Ephesians 5:18; Galatians 5:16, 25.

115 Romans 8:37; Colossians 1:13; Hebrews 2:14.

116 Romans 5:8.

117 Sprinkle, *Embodied*, 199–220.

118 Siegal, *Brainstorm*, 75–76.

119 1 Corinthians 13:7.

120 Shrier, *Irreversible Damage*, 163–171; Sprinkle, *Embodied*, 169.

121 Sprinkle, "Are Puberty Blockers…Laidlaw."

122 Shrier, *Irreversible Damage*, 163–71.

123 Hruz, et. al., "Growing Pains," 3, https://www.thenewatlantis.com/publications/growing-pains.

124 Psalm 139:13–14.

125 Luke 12:7.

126 Colossians 3:1–3.

127 Jeremiah 29:13.

128 Strength in Weakness Ministries, "Jennifer Konzen Interview" [Video] (2021), https://click.email.vimeo.com/core/?qs=e930fc-9b899868a83a994d5185fc0d71b34c84ea97e9f547f61662ffd65c1dae-440747a62511254ffa8bd5b95851fff0c1854f876655121b.

129 John 14:15.

130 1 John 4:19.

131 Exodus 3.

A free ebook edition is available with the purchase of this book.

To claim your free ebook edition:

1. Visit MorganJamesBOGO.com
2. Sign your name CLEARLY in the space
3. Complete the form and submit a photo of the entire copyright page
4. You or your friend can download the ebook to your preferred device

Morgan James
BOGO™

A **FREE** ebook edition is available for you
or a friend with the purchase of this print book.

CLEARLY SIGN YOUR NAME ABOVE

Instructions to claim your free ebook edition:
1. Visit MorganJamesBOGO.com
2. Sign your name CLEARLY in the space above
3. Complete the form and submit a photo
   of this entire page
4. You or your friend can download the ebook
   to your preferred device

Print & Digital Together Forever.

Snap a photo   Free ebook   Read anywhere

Printed in the USA
CPSIA information can be obtained
at www.ICGtesting.com
JSHW080148300824
69014JS00004BA/84